ENGLISH POETRY
From John Donne To Ted Hughes

ENGLISH POETRY

FORM JOHN DONNE TO TED HUGHES

Tomichan Matheikal

ATLANTIC
PUBLISHERS & DISTRIBUTORS (P) LTD

Published by

ATLANTIC

PUBLISHERS & DISTRIBUTORS (P) LTD

7/22, Ansari Road, Darya Ganj,
New Delhi-110002
Phones : +91-11-40775252, 23273880, 23275880, 23280451
Fax : +91-11-23285873
Web : www.atlanticbooks.com
E-mail : orders@atlanticbooks.com

Branch Office
5, Nallathambi Street, Wallajah Road,
Chennai-600002
Phones : +91-44-64611085, 32413319
E-mail : chennai@atlanticbooks.com

Printed in India at Nice Printing Press, A-33/3A, Site-IV, Industrial Area, Sahibabad, Ghaziabad, U.P.

PREFACE

The best literary works were written in poetic form until scientific rationalism triumphed over subjectivity and made us what Herbert Marcuse called "one-dimensional men" by reducing all 'truth' into objectivity. No student of literature can ignore the importance of poetry, however scientific and objective our civilization may have become.

This book is written primarily for students of literature. It introduces them to the major periods in the history of English literature up to and including the Modern period. The salient features of each period are discussed in the introductory chapters. The subsequent chapters present representative poems from each period. Each poem is discussed in detail in the critical appreciation that follows the poem. The purpose of the critical appreciation is to interpret the poem for the students of literature. The views of eminent critics have been given due place in each interpretation. This is done with the precise intention of making the student familiar not only with the poets but also with their important critics. It is hoped that every student of literature will find in this volume a valuable guide to English poetry.

I acknowledge my gratitude to M/s Atlantic Publishers and Distributors, New Delhi for enabling me to materialise this work in its present form.

TOMICHAN MATHEIKAL

CONTENTS

1

Metaphysical Poetry : An Introduction

Origin of the Term

John Dryden in his *Discourse of Satire* (1693) said rather pejoratively that Donne in his poetry "affects the metaphysics." What he meant was that Donne lavished into his poetry the terminology and abstruse arguments of the Scholastic philosophers so much so that he perplexed the minds of the fair sex when he should have endeavoured to conquer their hearts "with the softness of love." Nearly a century later Dr. Johnson perpetuated this derogatory appellation by sticking it to a school of poets ranging from Donne to Vaughan. What irritated the classical-minded Dr. Johnson was that the poems of Donne and his school did not correspond with Aristotle's denomination of poetry as "an imitative art." Thanks to Dr. Johnson, the label 'Metaphysical Poets' came to be applied to a group of diverse seventeenth century poets whose poems, whether secular or religious, have but certain similarities.

Characteristics of Metaphysical Poetry

Diverse as the poets of the Metaphysical school are, the search for a common Metaphysical weltanschauung (worldview) is destined to end in futility. However, many similarities have been traced in their poetic style and way of organising the thought. The characteristics common to this school of poets are described below :

1. Ratiocination

Ratiocination is methodical and logical reasoning. In most Metaphysical poems there is much ratiocination, "a motion of ideas towards determined ends in such a way that an air of logic is maintained in order to persuade" (Earl Miner). The process relies upon various means such as analogies, similitudes, arguments and proofs. The ratiocination in Donne's 'Death Be Not Proud,' for instance, consists in the arguments provided by the poet why death should not be proud. Another poem of Donne, 'The Flea,' contains a well-known example of the typical Metaphysical ratiocination. The poet argues that the flea which sucked the blood of two lovers has established a sacred relationship between the lovers, and itself metamorphosed into something sacred :

> This flea is you and I, and this
> Our marriage bed, and marriage temple is;

tells the poet to his beloved. Hence, killing the flea will not only be a triple murder but a sacrilege too.

"A fundamental way in which the ideas work in Metaphysical poetry is through 'definition' or 'identification,'" says Earl Miner. A concept is defined or identified as such and such. The whole ratiocination in the poem is based on that definition or identification, and is worked out through the various means mentioned above. The persuasive power of the arguments in 'The Flea,' for example, comes from the definition of the flea as "the marriage bed" and "marriage temple" of the pair of lovers. Similarly the sun is defined as a "Busy old fool" in 'The Sun Rising,' and man is defined as "a little world made cunningly" in 'I am a little world.'

2. Thought and Feeling

In the process of the intellectual ratiocination of the Metaphysical poetry, feeling has its appropriate place. Thought and feeling fuse into a peculiar union in Metaphysical poetry. This fusion is what T.S. Eliot called "the unified sensibility," although for Eliot "feeling" is not emotion, but a kind of sensation, to be felt "as immediately as the odour of a rose." Eliot's theory notwithstanding, in Metaphysical poetry there are emotions and they are shaped and expressed by logical reasoning. But words which are typically poetical are avoided by Metaphysical poets, because such words possess accumulated emotion and may awaken in us dormant emotions and memories. The Metaphysical quest is to produce a new sensibility in us, a new reaction to the reality described by the poet.

3. Conceits

In their endeavour to create a new poetic sensibility, the Metaphysical poets struck upon a strategy which is strikingly characteristic of their poetry in general: the use of conceits. A conceit is a comparison between two things which are in fact very unlike. As Helen Gardner says, "a comparison becomes a conceit when we are made to concede likeness while being strongly conscious of unlikeness."

There are two kinds of conceits :

(i) Short Conceit. The comparison in a short conceit can be applied only in the given context.

e.g., Cartwright's description of mction without progression :

Motion as in a mill
Is busy standing still.

In order to appreciate this comparison, we need to suppress our memory of other features of mills, and think of the one feature projected by the poet: motion without displacement.

(ii) Extended Conceit. The comparison in an extended conceit is an elaborate attempt to 'prove' the likeness between two things. They may start from a comparison which is far from the obvious but is subsequently and gradually made clear. Or they may start from an obvious comparison and then make us accept further resemblances in detail after detail.

4. Use of Wit

The conceits are generally employed in Metaphysical poetry in order to prove a point. The far-fetched comparisons come from all the various branches of knowledge that existed in the contemporary period. Relying so much upon intellectual ideas is what we mean by metaphysical use of wit, although the novelty of such ideas (which was another meaning of 'wit' in the seventeenth century) in Metaphysical poetry cannot be ignored. The Metaphysical poetry is often replete with allusions to such branches of knowledge as philosophy, medicine, politics, commerce, law, religion, war and military affairs.

5. Paradox

Paradox is an apparently self-contradictory or absurd statement, which turns out to have a valid meaning. It is a frequent incidental device in Metaphysical poetry, sometimes associated with conceits, sometimes occurring in witty argumentative stanzas.

e.g., Donne, in his Holy Sonnet XIV, asks God to destroy him so that he may be rejuvenated.

> Batter my heart, three person'd God; ...
> ... That I may rise and stand, o'erthrow me, and bend
> Your force to break, blow, burn and make me new.

Sometimes, the paradox gives an epigrammatic conciseness to the lines.

e.g., The grave's a fine and private place,
But none, I think, do there embrace.

(*Marvell*, '*To His Coy Mistress*')

6. Abrupt Opening

Dramatic opening is another characteristic of metaphysical poetry, whether the poet is speaking to his mistress, addressing God, setting a scene, or describing something.

e.g., For God's sake hold your tongue, and let me love

(*Donne*, '*The Canonization*')

> Go, and catch a falling star,
> Get with child a mandrake root,

(*Donne*, '*Song*')

> I struck the board, and cry'd, No more.
> I will abroad.

(*Herbert*, '*The Collar*')

7. Colloquial Style

Much of Metaphysical poetry is colloquial in diction as it is undecorative and untraditional in imagery and personal in tone. The Metaphysical poets prefer words in everyday use. In the words of Joan Bennett, they "use the natural language of men when they are soberly engaged in commerce or in scientific speculation, so that the words themselves, apart from their meaning in the context, have no repercussions." The colloquial diction gives a muscular rhythm to the poem.

8. Humour

"Almost all Metaphysical poems have an edge of dry humour to them, which does not invalidate what they say, but perhaps sobers it, and makes it more sensible" (J. Hunter). The smile produced by Metaphysical humour is subtle. The humour also helps to control or moderate the extremes of emotion, as does the colloquial style.

9. Religion and Metaphysical Poetry

The three Metaphysical poems included in this volume are all religious poems. Hence this note on religion and Metaphysical poetry.

In the early seventeenth century Calvinist theology was by and large the orthodox creed of English Protestantism: it dominated the Church of England. Calvinism emphasised God's eternal decrees, along with His initiative and grace which enable man's salvation. It stressed the absolute divine sovereignty and power and the notion of divine predestination, whereby salvation or damnation depends solely on God's will.

The harshness of the Calvinist theology, with its persistent emphasis on human depravity and sinfulness, could generate acute anxiety, doubt and restlessness. Calvinism expelled such intermediaries as priests between God and man's soul. No sacrament, no religious ceremony could provide the divine grace needed to assure one's salvation. "With its emphasis on the individual's personal relation to God, Protestantism could thus make God seem more awesomely distant and yet also bring Him more awesomely close" (David Loewenstein). Most of the agony, intense introspection and the simultaneous trust in God seen in the religious poems of the seventeenth century owe themselves to the impact of Calvinism on the believers.

Definition of Metaphysical Poetry

It is not easy to define Metaphysical poetry. However, a descriptive definition, as provided by Frank J. Warnke, is given here in conclusion to this discussion.

Metaphysical poetry is "a kind of poetry created in England during the first two thirds of the seventeenth century, distinguished by a radical use of conceited imagery, rational or argumentative structure, a specifically intellectual emphasis manifesting itself usually in a non-sensuous texture, a language — sometimes colloquial, sometimes learned — from which all traces of special poetic diction have been purged, a markedly dramatic tone, and a preoccupation, in both amorous and devotional poetry, with themes of transcendence and aspiration."

2

Death Be Not Proud

JOHN DONNE (1572-1631)

Death be not proud, though some have called thee
Mighty and dreadful, for thou art not so,
For, those, whom thou think'st, thou dost overthrow,
Die not, poor death, nor yet canst thou kill me.

From rest and sleep, which but thy pictures be,
Much pleasure, then from thee, much more must flow,
And soonest our best men with thee do go,
Rest of their bones, and soul's delivery.

Thou art slave to fate, chance, kings, and desperate men,
And dost with poison, war, and sickness dwell,
And poppy, or charms can make us sleep as well,
And better than thy stroke; why swell'st thou then?

One short sleep past, we wake eternally,
And death shall be no more; death, thou shalt die.

Critical Appreciation

'Death Be Not Proud' is one of the nineteen poems in Donne's Holy Sonnets, the anthology which contains the core of the poet's religious verse. Most of the sonnets are written with as much passion as are the poet's celebrated love-poems. But the passion in these 'divine poems' is more complex; "it is that mixture of hope and anguish that characterises the religious man searching for the right relationship with God, aware both of his own unworthiness and of God's infinite greatness" (David Daiches).

The sequence of six sonnets on death and judgement, of which 'Death Be Not Proud' is the last, is a poignant expression of the poet's agonising memory of his own sins as well as of his immense trust in the redemptive power of Christ, the Son of God.

> O God, Oh! of thine only worthy blood,
> And my tears, make a heavenly Lethean flood,
> And drown in it my sin's black memory.
>
> (*If Poisonous Minerals*)

"Donne's poetry is always quick with fear;" says Jim Hunter (*The Metaphysical Poets*). Most of the holy sonnets reveal an implicit fear of death. However, the tone of 'Death Be Not Proud' is one of remonstration rather than of fear. The poem opens with a direct chastisement of death for its haughtiness over the mightiness and dreadfulness ascribed to it by some people. The poet asserts bluntly that death is neither mighty nor dreadful. It is sheer vanity on its part if death thinks that those who are overthrown by it are killed once and for all. Death is not the end of human beings on earth and it will not be the end of the poet either.

In the holy sonnets, 'Oh My Black Soul!' and 'This is My Play's Last Scene,' Donne compares human life on earth to a pilgrimage. When the pilgrimage is completed, the pilgrim has to return to his original abode where life is eternal. Hence, death is merely the end of a sojourn.

Relaxation and sleep are shadows of death in so far as they provide a respite, however, brief, from the worries and cares of life. If these can provide so much pleasure, then the ultimate relief given by death should be much greater. Sooner or later even "our best men" opt for this relief. At any rate, death has nothing to be proud of because even when it steals the best men, it is only doing them a service by giving rest to their tired bones and salvation to their immortal souls.

Death is subject to the arbitrariness of "fate, chance, kings, and desperate men." All these can cause somebody's death according to their whim and fancy. That which is a slave to such arbitrariness has nothing to be proud of. Moreover, death's dwelling places are in such pernicious things or events as "poison, war and sickness."

Returning to the motif of sleep and relaxation, Donne once again asserts that drugs and charms can induce in us much better sleep than death can. So death has absolutely no reason to swell with pride over the fact that it provides rest to man. The argument now seems contradictory as the poet had earlier spoken of death as the ultimate relief. The contradiction owes itself partly to Donne's fear of death submerged beneath the bold facade of challenge put up by the poet (see note on Religion and Metaphysical Poetry in the Introduction). However, it is not a flaw if we take into consideration the paradoxical nature of the whole argument which reaches a climax in the last two lines.

The final blow of the poet's crushing ratiocination on death comes in the last two lines :

> One short sleep past, we wake eternally,
> And death shall be no more; death, thou shalt die.

Death is not a conqueror. It is merely an instrument which liberates man from his mortal body and elevates him into the world of eternity where death has no power whatever. Hence, death is self-destructive. When it kills, it is dying itself; it is transporting man's life to where that life will be beyond the faintest influence of death.

Coupling passion with reason is characteristic of all metaphysical poetry, particularly of Donne's poems. The personification of death is addressed with downright passionate severity in 'Death Be Not Proud,' and the reasons for the admonitions are listed with logic that is meticulous despite the paradoxes. The passionate ratiocination gradually strips death of all its ascribed mightiness, and finally leaves it in a paradoxical situation : "death, thou shalt die."

Paradox is an incidental device which occurs quite frequently in the argumentative stanzas of much Metaphysical verse. It adds to the persuasive power of the ratiocination.

3

Virtue

GEORGE HERBERT (1593-1633)

Sweet day, so cool, so calm, so bright,
The bridal of the earth and sky :
The dew shall weep thy fall tonight;
For thou must die.

Sweet rose, whose hue angry and brave,
Bids the rash gazer wipe his eye :
Thy root is ever in its grave,
And thou must die.

Sweet spring, full of sweet days and roses,
A box where sweets compacted lie;
My music shows ye have your closes,
And all must die.

Only a sweet and virtuous soul,
Like season'd timber, never gives;
But though the whole world turns to coal,
Then chiefly lives.

Critical Appreciation

George Herbert's poem, 'Virtue', contrasts the mortality of all natural phenomena, however "sweet" they may be, with the immortality of the human soul that is both "sweet and virtuous."

The first line of each of the first three stanzas begins "in a tone of even, reflective enjoyment" (M. M. Mahood) of the sensuous beauty of the phenomenon under consideration. The second line reinforces that one by a striking image. The last two lines all but negate the sweetness and sensuality established in the previous lines by the figurative statement about the inevitable end of all natural phenomena : they all "must die."

Herbert was a pastor who, in his poems, dealt with the great Christian themes which he taught with devoted simplicity in spite of the technical polishness of the verse. His poetry works on a peculiar "combination of shock and repose.... There is conflict in the poetry, yet there is calm trust; disturbed speculation yet simple faith; ingenious language ... and the gentle simplicity of a wise and compassionate preacher" (David Daiches). All these characteristics are illustrated by his brilliant poem, 'Virtue.'

Apparently a simple poem, 'Virtue' develops ingeniously into an arresting piece of art on closer examination. Louis L Martz compares this poem to a classical building. "As in the design of a classical building, what seems at first so clear and obvious grows from a very subtle convergence of lines and perspectives. Such art as this is founded upon security, can arise only from security." The security is provided by the very structure of the poem, and is in perfect harmony with the theme.

The day and the rose, two natural phenomena chosen by the poet for special consideration, are "sweet." The word 'sweet' had delicate, fragrant associations in the seventeenth century, "but without any suggestion of un-masculine or feeble feeling; it was both strong and delicate..." (Jim Hunter). The day which has the solemn masculine characteristics of coolness, calmness and brightness is also the delicate bride of the entire nature comprising the earth and its environment, the sky. The ultimate fate of the day, however, is to submit itself to the inevitable flow of time and come to a close. Nature's tears will drop as dew when the day yields to the unremitting power of death.

Like the day, the rose too is "sweet." The flower flaunts its colour with a masculine aggressiveness and bravery. But its delicacy can fill an admirer's eyes with tears, because its sweetness is ephemeral. The rose is rooted in the earth into which the flower will finally fall, never to rise again.

A new bud may blossom on the rose just as a new day will replace the bygone day. However, all these days and all these roses which together will constitute the whole "sweet" season of spring is also destined to meet the same fate : death. The spring season is compared to a box which contains all the fragrances ("sweets") of nature in a compact form. The poet adds that just as his own music, the music of this poem, is reaching its culmination ('close' is the concluding part of a musical piece; a cadence), so will the spring have its cadences.

The security of the poem, referred to by Martz, arises from various factors. The disparate elements of the first two stanzas, the days and the roses, are brought together into a single block in the spring of the third stanza : "Sweet spring, full of sweet days and roses." The rhymes of these three stanzas are carefully built too. The second and fourth lines of each stanza end rhyming with the word 'die,' a word which is repeated three times in these stanzas. The oscillation between 'sweet' and 'die' may indeed be an unsettling one. But this oscillation is soon brought to a firm and reassuring equilibrium in the last stanza. It is brought about by the shift in the position of "sweet," and the change in the rhyme, as much as by the spiritual content of the stanza.

When everything "sweet" "must die," there is one thing that is "sweet" and is immortal too : it is the "virtuous soul," which like "season'd timber" will not yield to the ravages of time. Even seasoned timber is not the right metaphor for the virtuous soul, as the former will turn to ashes too some time or the other. Everything material will perish, but the virtuous soul will live on for ever. It is virtue alone, thus, that is immortal and hence the significance of the title of the poem.

(Author is indebted to Louis L. Martz's essay, 'The Action of the Self : Devotional Poetry in the Seventeenth Century,' for many of the views expressed here.)

4

The Retreat

HENRY VAUGHAN (1621-95)

Happy those early days! when I
Shin'd in my Angel-infancy.
Before I understood this place
Appointed for my second race,
Or taught my soul to fancy ought
But a white, celestial thought,
When yet I had not walked above
A mile, or two, from my first love,
And looking back (at that short space,)
Could see a glimpse of his bright face;
When on some gilded cloud, or flower
My gazing soul would dwell an hour,
And in those weaker glories spy
Some shadows of eternity,
Before I taught my tongue to wound
My conscience with a sinful sound,
Or had the black art to dispense
A several sin to every sense,
And felt through all this fleshly dress
Bright shoots of everlastingness.

O how I long to travel back
And tread again that ancient track!
That I might once more reach that plain,
Where first I left my glorious train,
From whence th' enlightened spirit sees

That shady city of palm trees;
But (ah!) my soul with too much stay
Is drunk, and staggers in the way.
Some men a forward motion love,
But I by backward steps would move,
And when this dust falls to the urn
In that state I came, return.

Critical Appreciation

'The Retreat' is a succinct expression of Henry Vaughan's firm belief that in childhood man is pure and good, and hence in a unique relationship with God. Childhood, for Vaughan, "is the state of innocence, and maturity is corrupting" (Jim Hunter). The poem also contains the Neo-platonic idea that the soul loses its purity by its descent into the body. The material world distances man from God in two ways : by its being a degree inferior to the world of pure spirits, and by its corruptibility. Vaughan, as David Daiches says, "is conscious of a veil which separates time from eternity, man from God, and is constantly seeking for ways to penetrate it."

'The Retreat' is largely about the sad fate of man destined to live behind the veil that separates him from God. The poem opens with a recollection of the poet's childhood when the poet was exuberant as he could then be in the presence of God because of his angelic innocence. He had not then been corrupted by the mundane world to which he is sent to run his "second race," the first being the prenatal existence in paradise with God. During childhood his soul enjoyed a divine purity of vision ("a white, celestial thought"). He had not then walked away from God, his "first love." He was always in the vicinity of God so that at any moment he could turn back and have a fulfilling glimpse of God's bright face. Some golden cloud or a bright flower would capture the attention of the poet so much that he could contemplate on them...for a long time, and perceive images of eternity in them.

Those were the days when the poet had not been corrupted by this world, when his tongue knew not a sinful word, when he had not acquired the black magic of this world which can make every sense organ guilty of a separate sin. On the other hand, those were the days when he could feel through his body the pulsation ("bright shoots") of eternity.

The corrupting influences of this world, regarded as black magic by the poet, are in diametric contrast to the "white, celestial thought" of the childhood purity. Both have a charming power on the human being. But man, being a composite of both spirit and matter who has his existence in this world of matter, is pulled more and more away from the world of the spirit.

The second part of the poem expresses the poet's irrepressible longing to return to his childhood innocence.

> O how I long to travel back
> And tread again that ancient track!

It is only such a return, feels the poet, that can place him once again in an integral communion with the ultimate reality, the spiritual world, from where he has wandered away, not "A mile, or two," but much too far. It is from "that plain" of childhood innocence that man derives enlightenment, the vision of the celestial city.

The celestial city is described as "That shady city of palm trees" by the poet. It is "shady" because it is not material. There is a poem entitled 'The Palm Tree', written by Vaughan. It is a meditation on the traditional emblem of the tree which is "pressed and bowed" with "weights (like death/And sin)," but the more he's bent/The more he grows." The tree is then related to the palm tree used in the building of Solomon's Temple, the tree of immortality in Eden, the crown of palm for victors in the fight against evil, and with "the patience of the Saints." Thus, the palm tree has a spiritual significance for Vaughan.

The poet's attempt to return to the "plain" of childhood innocence is rendered immensely difficult by the very fact of his having stayed for too long in the mundane world of the adult. He has already been so corrupted ("drunk") that he can only "stagger." The poem concludes with an apparently dialectical statement :

> Some men a forward motion love,
> But I by backward steps would move.

For the poet, however, there is no dialectics. His longing to return to the state he came from, the state of childhood innocence, is sincere and earnest.

Vaughan was a mystic and much of his poetry was composed on religious themes. He was so much seized with the idea of childhood innocence, and the child's recollection of prenatal glory that, as Jim Hunter says, "if it were possible to be still a child, he would quickly choose it" : "And by mere playing go to Heaven ('Childhood')."

Attempts have been made to compare Vaughan with Wordsworth, as the latter too believed in the glorious prenatal existence of man with God. However, such comparisons are unwarranted. Vaughan differs from Wordsworth especially in that Wordsworth celebrates the earthly life while Vaughan laments the baseness of earthly life. There are indeed Romantic streaks in Vaughan. "His subject-matter is that which is *evoked* rather than identified and argued over" (Hunter). His consciousness lives in a different milieu, as is the case with the Romantic poets. Nevertheless, Vaughan is not a Romantic poet, since the memory of the moments of illumination that he is endeavouring to maintain differs substantially from the Romantic flights of imagination.

It may also not be completely right to label Vaughan as a Metaphysical poet. He was indeed influenced by George Herbert. But his mature poetry is significantly different from Herbert's, as it is from any other Metaphysical poet's. To quote Hunter again, "...whereas Metaphysical poetry always links reason and emotion, and puts up a logical front, there are times in Vaughan where logic is far off, and we are presented not with meditation but with vision or intuition, unexplained and inexplicable."

5

The Age of Reason and Sensibility : An Introduction

Science and scientific rationalism began to hold sway over people's mind and imagination from about the middle of the seventeenth century and its influence on literature continued until the Romantics rebelled against it. The scientific temper radically altered people's attitudes in general. Many age-old beliefs and values faced a threat. The world ceased to be an object of contemplation, a source of the sense of mystery and awe, and came to be seen as a complex of forces to be studied and measured scientifically. The mechanistic and deterministic materialism advocated by Thomas Hobbes (1583-1579) dampened the spiritual and ethical quest of the people.

The attitudinal change had its effect on the poetry of the period. It sapped the poet's trust in imagination and intuition. Whatever savoured of the irrational became anathema. Rationalism and scientific empiricism cannot produce inspired poetry. It is only natural that the poets of this period looked to men and their manners for the subject of their poetry. "Poetry became to a large degree public, occasional., mundane, social," as Douglas Bush says. Quite naturally, much of the poetry of the period, at least the best of it, was satire. The predominance of satire owed itself also to the supremacy that town life was gaining over country life. The scandals, artificial fashions and squabbles of the cultured town dwellers were grist to the satirist's mill.

The age emphasised the value of manners and decorum in public life. Poetry too became self-conscious. Matter, form and style became subjects of conscious consideration. Good sense and good taste were highly valued. The conscious attempt to maintain decorum in poetry led the poets to classical conventions. This period is also known as the neo-classical period. Some of the traits of the contemporary poetry such as clarity of thought and expression, suppression of emotion, restraint, exaltation of reason and adherence to established rules and conventions owe as much to the classical spirit as to the scientific temper of the period.

Douglas Bush points out that the key-word of the literature of the age is "nature.' He defines nature as "the rational, civilized traditional norm in every department of human activity." Pope argues in his *Essay on Criticism* that poets imitate nature. The supreme imitators of nature were the classical writers. Hence, "to copy nature is to copy them" (Pope). In simple words, the advice to "follow nature" enjoined upon the poets the duty to reproduce the day-to-day life of men. While adherence to nature, that is, to customs and conventions, was hailed as a virtue, deviations from it were seen as vices or follies. The best mode for presenting these vices and follies was satire.

The main areas of the satire of the period were man and society, religion and politics, literature and writers. Like all satire, the seventeenth and eighteenth century satire devoted itself to chastisement and correction of the vices and follies of men. Egged on by the scientific temper and the classical moorings, the satirists of the period strove to attain universality by writing about general human vices and follies. Hence we find both universality and particularity in much of the satire of this period.

Two great verse satirists of the period were John Dryden and Alexander Pope. One of the chief features of Dryden's satire is that there is no affectation of great moral indignation in his attack. He wielded the weapon of contempt rather than of indignation. His intention was to laugh at the follies of men rather than to declaim against their vices.

Dryden exercised moderation in both detail and tone while satirising persons. He is seldom vituperative or even exhaustive. He chooses to leave out many details and confines himself to generalisations instead of making specific charges. His moderation even while presenting a thoroughbred opportunist like Shaftesbury can be seen in the extract included in this volume. However, on rare occasions, Dryden can also be mean in his attack as seen in the case of his utterance about Shaftesbury's son, again found in this volume.

Yet another quality of Dryden's satiric portraits is that they are neither too general nor too particular. His sketches are at the same time types and individuals. For example, Achitophel is both the usual political conspirer and a unique individual.

Dryden made use of the heroic couplet with great dexterity. His verse reveals a remarkably varied cadence. Its strong antithesis (*e.g.*, "Resolved to ruin or to rule the state," "With public zeal to cancel private crimes") and sarcasm (*e.g.*, "Who stand confirmed in stupidity," "But Shadwell never deviates into sense") give a sharp edge to the satire.

Pope was pre-eminently a satirist, though he wrote other kinds of poems too. His satire was of two kinds : (1) general, as in *The Rape of the Lock* in which the faults and foibles of women in general were satirised and (2) individual and personal as in *The Dunciad* and *The Imitations of Horace*. The second kind was used by Pope to attack his rivals. The attacks were often virulent, malicious and scurrilous. In the words of Bush, "Pope hurries along with a machine-gun in his hands, discharging gibes and aphorisms with equal briskness." There certainly are many features of his characters which belong to human nature in general so that the portraits do not end up in total topicality. Yet, unlike Dryden, "Pope is likely to focus his eye so sharply upon his sitters that the typical is more submerged in the individual" (Bush).

Pope, like Dryden, was an expert in handling the heroic couplet. It was the medium of his satire.

6

Portrait of Achitophel

(from *Absalom and Achitophel*, Part I)

JOHN DRYDEN (1631-1700)

Of these the false Achitophel was first :
A name to all succeeding ages curst.
For close designs, and crooked counsels fit;
Sagacious, bold, and turbulent of wit.
Restless, unfixt in principles and place;
In power unpleased, impatient of disgrace.
A fiery soul, which working out its way,
Fretted the pigmy-body to decay :
And o'er inform'd the tenement of clay.
A daring pilot in extremity;
Pleased with the danger, when the waves were high
He sought the storms; but for a calm unfit,
Would steer too nigh the sands, to boast his wit.
Great wits are sure to madness near allied;
And thin partitions do their bounds divide :
Else why should he, with wealth and honour blest,
Refuse his age the needful hours of rest?
Punish a body which he could not please;
Bankrupt of life, yet prodigal of ease?
And all to leave, what with his toil he won,
To that unfeather'd two-legg'd thing, a son :
Got, while his soul did huddled notions try;
And born a shapeless lump, like anarchy.
In friendship false, implacable in hate :

Resolved to ruin or to rule the state.
To compass this, the triple bond he broke;
The pillars of the public safety shook :
And fitted Israel for a foreign yoke.
Then seized with fear, yet still affecting fame,
Usurp'd a patriot's all-atoning name.
So easy still it proves in factious times,
With public zeal to cancel private crimes :
How safe is treason, and how sacred ill,
When none can sin against the people's will :
Where crowds can wink; and no offence be known,
Since in another's guilt they find their own.
Yet, fame deserved, no enemy can grudge;
The statesman we abhor, but praise the Judge.
In Israel's courts ne'er sat an Abbethdin
With more discerning eyes, or hands more clean :
Unbribed, unsought, the wretched to redress;
Swift of dispatch, and easy of access.
Oh, had he been content, to serve the Crown,
With virtues only proper to the Gown;
Or, had the rankness of the soil been freed
From cockle, that oppressed the noble seed :
David, for him his tuneful harp had strung,
And heaven had wanted one immortal song.
But wild ambition loves to slide, not stand;
And fortune's ice prefers to virtue's land :
Achitophel, grown weary to possess
A lawful fame, and lazy happiness;
Disdained the golden fruit to gather free,
And lent the crowd his arm to shake the tree.

Notes

line

3. close designs : secret plans
4. sagacious : shrewd; turbulent of wit : chaotic of imagination
5. place : office or position

9. o'er inform'd : animated excessively; over-worked tenement of clay : body; tenement : house

10. pilot : captain

11-13. Achitophel deliberately took risks to exhibit his ability. He was like a captain who sailed his ship into the interior sea on stormy days, and who sailed close to the shore on calm days, both risky things to do.

14. There is no genius without some mixture of madness.

15. The line that divides genius from madness is thin.

21-23. The reference is to Shafetsbury's son, Anthony, born two weeks before his father trying out confused notions, joined a committee of Cromwell's Parliament in 1652. "A two-legged, unfeathered animal" is a supposedly Platonic definition of man. The reference to Anthony as "a shapeless lump, like anarchy" is unjustified as Anthony was a handsome man.

26. the triple bond : the alliance England made with Holland and Sweden in 1667/8. The second Treaty with France (1670) ended that alliance. Shaftesbury was a signatory to the Second Treaty.

28. foreign yoke : France

33. ill : crime

37-48. These twelve lines of praise were added in the second edition of the poem, published after the acquittal of Shaftesbury.

39. Abbethdin : 'Father of the court of justice,' one of the two presiding judges of the Jewish civil court. Shaftesbury was Lord Chancellor for a number of years.

44. Gown : profession of law

45. rankness : fertility

46. cockle : weed

47-48. David would have sung his praises instead of writing a psalm (hymn to God), and so heaven would have had one immortal song the less.

49-50. Ambitious people are like ice-skaters. They take risks and may follow devious paths in order to achieve their goals. But virtuous people stand steady on the solid ground of their virtues. Macaulay traces the origin of this couplet to the frontispiece of Knolle's *History of the Turks* :

Greatness on goodness loves to slide, not stand
And leaves for fortune's ice virtue's firm land.

51. to possess : of possessing

53. golden fruit : political benefits

51-54. Weary and disdainful of the just fame and easy life he had, Shaftesbury posed as a supporter of the people and opposed the King in order to reap political benefits.

Political background

Charles II was restored to the throne of England in 1660. His wife was Catherine of Braganza, a Spanish princess. They had no children. Hence it was taken for granted that James, Duke of York and brother of Charles II, would succeed to the throne. However, James was a Catholic, and there existed a great prejudice against Catholics in those days. It was assumed that the Catholics were in league with France and were awaiting the opportunity to establish Catholicism in England. Consequently, the Catholics in England were oppressed in many ways.

The question of succession became a much debated issue with the advent of the two parties : the Whigs and the Tories. The Whigs pressed for the exclusion of the Duke of York from the right of succession. Their leader was the Earl of Shaftesbury. The Tories, in their eagerness to please the King, lent their support to the right of the Duke of York to succeed to the throne, because the King was favourably disposed to the Duke. The Tory party had the backing of the aristocracy and the clergy of England.

One of the Whig propagandas against the Catholics was the notorious Popish Plot. Under the leadership of Titus Oates, it was propagated that the Catholics were plotting to murder the King. The Earl of Shaftesbury was quick to exploit the situation.

Shaftesbury had a chequered career. As a young man, he was a Member of Parliament and held many important posts under the King. He switched over to the parliamentary side in 1644, five years before the royal regime was usurped and the Commonwealth rule was established. For some time he posed as an enemy of the Royalists. But soon he started an intrigue with the exiled King and his supporters, because the British citizens had become more and more disillusioned with the Commonwealth rule. He was one of the twelve persons who went to Holland to invite the King back to the throne, in 1660.

Shaftesbury was made Lord Ashley as a reward for his apparent loyalty to the King. Later, when he became Lord Chancellor he was reputed to be just and honest. But he was a thorough-bred opportunist, always anxious to advance his own interests. His machinations to rise in power locked him into a sharp tussle with the Duke of York. As a result, the office of the Lord Chancellor was taken away from him in 1673. Consequently, he became a sworn enemy of the Duke of York and of Catholicism.

One of Shaftesbury's tricks was to gain the confidence of the people on behalf of the Duke of Monmouth, the illegitimate son of Charles II. Monmouth was projected as "the great confessor for the Protestant religion." Shaftesbury was initially successful in rousing the people's ire, against the King and the Duke of York. The situation became critical with the propaganda about the Popish Plot (1679).

After more than two years of crisis and of executions for complicity in the Popish Plot, the tide began to turn in favour of the King. Shaftesbury was arrested on charges of high treason and was committed to the Tower.

Absalom and Achitophel, said to have been written at the request of the King, was published just before the trial of Shaftesbury with the design of prejudicing the jury. However, Shaftesbury was acquitted by the jury which consisted of Protestants.

The poem recounts the story of the exclusionist campaign, the Popish Plot, and Shaftesbury's seduction of Monmouth, with character-sketches of the King's enemies and his friends, in an elaborate allegorical application of the Biblical history of David, Absalom and Achitophel.

Biblical Background

David (d. 962 B.C.) was the king of Judah and Israel. It was he who founded the Jewish royal dynasty at Jerusalem. Absalom was one of David's sons. Absalom's sister, Tamar, was forced into sexual union by Amnon, her step-brother. Infuriated by the violation of his sister, Absalom killed Amnon and fled to the country of Geshur, where he lived for three years.

Absalom was brought back to Jerusalem by the efforts of Joab who interceded with David on the young man's behalf. However, David refused to let Absalom live with him in the palace. Two years later Absalom was admitted to the king's presence, once again through the intercession of Joab. He was given a chariot, some horses and fifty men.

Absalom began to win favour with the people of Israel by telling them that he would dispense justice to them the way the king never did, if only he had the power to do so. Having thus secured the confidence of a sizeable section of the Israelites, Absalom went to Hebron pretending to be fulfilling a vow he had made to God. However, his trip to Hebron was the culmination of the intricate conspiracy he had been hatching against the king. He had sent secret messages to the people of Israel that as soon as they heard the sound of trumpet they should cry out : "Absalom is king at Hebron!"

While in Hebron, Absalom gathered a large number of supporters. David's counsellor, Achitophel; too joined him. David, having heard of Absalom's intentions, fled from Jerusalem. Absalom returned to Jerusalem and, following Achitophel's counsel, took charge not only of the throne but of his father's concubines as well, the latter of the actions being in order to prove to the people that he was absolutely supplanting his father in kingship. Although Achitophel offered to pursue David and kill him, Hushai advised Absalom against such an action as David was an expert in war and had very valiant men with him. Hushai suggested that Absalom himself went to battle. However, this was a treachery on the part of Hushai as he informed David of Absalom's strategies. Thus David was able to defeat Absalom's men.

Achitophel was dejected on learning that Absalom had not accepted his counsel. He committed suicide.

Absalom was caught up among the branches of an oak as his mule passed under the tree during the battle. Although David had ordered that Absalom should be protected during the battle, Joab and his men killed Absalom while he was trapped among the oak branches.

The parallels between the biblical and historical personalities

David	:	Charles II
Absalom	:	Duke of Monmouth (James Scott), illegitimate son of Charles II.
Achitophel	:	Earl of Shaftesbury (Anthony Ashley-Cooper)
Israel	:	England
Jews	:	the English
Jerusalem	:	London
Hebron	:	Scotland
Jebusites	:	Catholics

Critical Appreciation

The Popish Plot had wreaked a lot of havoc in the century. Many people tried to take advantage of the situation. There were some people who had been raised by the King to high status in the parliament, but were ungrateful. One of them was the treacherous Achitophel whose name will be cursed by generations to come. He was skilled in hatching plots. He misguided people with "crooked counsels." Shrewd and bold though he was, his imagination remained chaotic. He had no firm principles. He was as irritable as disgruntled. The excessive zeal of his soul took its toll on his frail body and made him emaciated.

Nevertheless, Achitophel was a courageous leader in critical situations. Hazards emboldened him. Dryden compares him to the captain of a ship who loves to sail deep into the sea on a stormy day, and who steers his ship close to the sands on calm days.

Achitophel deliberately took risks to boast about his dexterity in handling dangerous situations. Genius is "near allied" to madness, says Dryden commenting on Achitophel's nature.

If it were not indeed madness, why would a man like Achitophel who had been blessed with wealth and honour, jeopardise his senile body instead of providing it with the much needed rest? Achitophel was reaching the end of his life and yet was searching for more and more pleasures. Whatever he would thus achieve with great pain, would all in the end be bequeathed to his son, "born a shapeless lump, like anarchy."

Shaftesbury's son, Anthony, was born two weeks before Shaftesbury joined a committee of Cromwell's Parliament in 1652. Shaftesbury's political decisions were matters of convenience and opportunism rather than of principles, and hence referring to them satirically (*e.g.*, trying out "huddled notions") is justified. However, the reference to Anthony as a mis-shapened man is quite unfair as he was a fairly handsome man.

Achitophel's crimes and vices are further investigated. He was deceitful even towards his friends and "implacable in hate." The craze for power made him resolute, but the resolution was either "to ruin or to rule the state." In this part of the portrait, as in many other parts of the poem, Achitophel is being compared to Milton's Satan. "Implacable in hate" echoes the defiance of Satan pledging "study of revenge, immortal hate" (*Paradise Lost*, I, 107). Achitophel's resolution to rule or ruin reflects Satan's determination about God's creation :

either with Hell fire
To waste his whole creation, or possess
All as our own...

(*Paradise Lost*, II, 364-6)

As A W Hoffman points out, the imagery of *Absalom and Achitophel* takes up the themes of God and man. "The imagery at an early stage," says Hoffman, "introduces faint suggestions of David as God and of Absalom as Adam and of the events in paradise." Achitophel is the Satan who tempts man to rebel against God.

Achitophel, in order to feather his nest, broke the "triple bond." The triple bond that Dryden speaks of is the alliance England made with Holland and Sweden in 1667. The Second Treaty with France (1670) ended that alliance. Shaftesbury was a signatory to that Treaty. However, Dryden's allegation that Shaftesbury enslaved the Protestant England to Catholic France is unjustified. Although Shaftesbury shared responsibility for involving England in war against Holland in 1672, he was not in the least aware of Charles's agreement with France that he would declare himself a Roman Catholic at an opportune moment.

Confused and confounded by the consequence of his own actions, Achitophel still managed to pose himself as a hero before the people by pretending to be a patriot. It is easy, comments Dryden, to negate one's "private crimes" by depicting them as patriotic deeds. When the country is facing a critical situation, even treason becomes safe; the traitor may come to be seen as an advocate of people's causes.

The satire in the portrait is mitigated by the twelve lines of praise (37-48) for Achitophel's merit as a judge. These twelve lines were added in the second edition of the poem, probably with an intention of placating Shaftesbury's feelings after his acquittal. At any rate, the praise is justified not only because Shaftesbury was much appreciated as Lord Chancellor but also because it makes the portrait more balanced.

If Achitophel was abhorrent as a statesman, he was praiseworthy as a judge. No better judge ever sat in Israel's courts. He was blessed with judiciousness and incorruptibility. He meted out justice impartially and swiftly. If only he remained content with his legal profession, the country would have gained much. If the evil growing like weeds in Achitophel's nature had not suppressed the development of the goodness in that soil, king David would have sung songs in praise of him although that might have reduced the number of psalms the king composed in praise of God.

Needless to say, wild ambition can never stand still. Ambitious people are like ice-skaters. They take risks and may follow devious paths in order to achieve their goals, while virtuous people stand steady on the solid ground of virtues. Achitophel, being ambitious, grew weary of possessing the rightful fame and the simple happiness it proffered. Disdaining the golden fruit, he joined the masses in the rebellion against the king in order to accrue whatever benefits he could in the process.

Satire in the Poem

Satire is the literary art of diminishing a subject by making it ridiculous and evoking towards it attitudes of amusement, contempt, indignation or scorn. Satires can be broadly classified as (i) formal or direct satire and (ii) indirect satire. In formal satire the satiric voice speaks out in the first person (*e.g.*, Pope's *Moral Essays*). Indirect satire is cast in the form of a narrative instead of direct address. One type of indirect satire is Menippean satire or Varronian satire of which *Absalom and Achitophel* is an example. Although Varronian satire attacks the vices and follies of persons concerned, there is in it a lack of moral indignation.

The portrait of Achitophel is a satirical delineation of Shaftesbury's political career. Like the other portraits in *Absalom and Achitophel*, this one is a brilliant example of Dryden's skill in careful and detailed description of a person's character. Dryden seldom transgresses the limits of moderation and sobriety. True, there are occasions, such as when he alludes to Shaftesbury's son, when his pen seems to run away with him. But such occasions are rare. On the whole, in the words of David Daiches, "The satire is not a savage black-and-white affair; the tone is more often amused than outraged, and if the villains are on the side of evil they nevertheless have interesting and even admirable qualities as men."

Shaftesbury's portrait "is a picture of a complex and tortured character" (Daiches). Shaftesbury as portrayed by Dryden is not simply a villain. The impression created is "one of twisted brilliance, of genius gone wrong,... rather than of simple evil or of little nastiness" (Daiches). Dryden's restraint in satirisation prevents his characters from ending up as caricatures; they are real-life persons with a mixture of good and evil in them. The good is appreciated as in the tribute paid to Shaftesbury's merits as a judge. The evil is not made a cause for moral indignation, but is only laughed at. Moral indignation arises from a feeling of self-righteousness which has no place in a work of satire. Dryden was of the opinion that no man should be labelled a villain or rogue, but may be made to "appear a fool, a blockhead or a knave without using any of these opprobrious terms." It is the spirit of good-humoured ridicule that he advocated.

The ridicule is not without sympathy. The lines, "Oh! had he been content..." gives a sense of virtue wasted and distorted. Shaftesbury was both a genius and a virtuous man. But, alas, a fallen angel too. It is the fall from loftiness that Dryden satirises. And the style he chose is that of the heroic couplet. The heroic couplet consists of lines of iambic pentameter which rhymes in pairs. A heroic poem is usually a long narrative poem on a great and serious subject, related in an elevated style, and centred on a heroic figure on whose actions depends the fate of a large number of people. Since *Absalom and Achitophel* is an allegory based on a historical and Biblical event, Dryden's choice of the heroic couplet is apt. As D. D. Brown says, "What gives the poem its distinctive quality is that within the heroic framework... everywhere the treatment of serious subjects is enlivened by touches of wit and humour."

7

Portrait of Sporus

ALEXANDER POPE (1688-1744)

Let Sporus tremble — "What? that thing of silk,
"Sporus, that mere white curd of ass's milk?
"Satire or sense alas! can Sporus feel?
"Who breaks a butterfly upon a wheel?"
Yet let me flap this bug with gilded wings,
This painted child of dirt that stinks and stings;
Whose buzz the witty and the fair annoys,
Yet wit ne'er tastes, and beauty ne'er enjoys,
So well-bred spaniels civilly delight
In mumbling of the game they dare not bite.
Eternal smiles his emptiness betray,
As shallow streams run dimpling all the way.
Whether in florid impotence he speaks,
And, as the prompter breathes, the puppet squeaks;
Or at the ear of Eve, familiar toad,
Half froth, half venom, spits himself abroad,
In puns, or politics, or tales, or lies,
Or spite, or smut, or rhymes, or blasphemies.
His wit all see-saw between that and this,
Now high, now low, now Master up, now Miss,
And he himself one vile antithesis.
Amphibious thing! that acting either part,
The trifling head, or the corrupted heart!
Fop at the toilet, flatt'rer at the board,
Now trips a lady, and now struts a lord.
Eve's tempter thus the Rabbins have expressed,

A cherub's face, a reptile all the rest;
Beauty that shocks you, parts that none will trust,
Wit that can creep, and pride that licks the dust.

Critical Appreciation

'Portrait of Sporus' is an extract from *Epistle to Dr. Arbuthnot* which Pope composed as the prologue to his satires and epistles. Dr. John Arbuthnot (1667-1735) was a leading physician of Pope's time. He was an intimate friend of Pope and Swift. In the Epistle, Pope settles some old scores with his adversaries, especially Addison, Colley Cibber, Ambrose Philips, John Dennis, Richard Bentley, Hervey, Welsted and Bubb Dodington.

In the extract given here Baron Hervey of Ickworth (1696-1743) is satirised in the character of Sporus. Sporus was the name of the eunuch-love of Nero, the Roman emperor. Hervey was a confidential man of Queen Anne. As a minister he supported Prime Minister Walpole. His crime against Pope was that he composed, together with Lady Mary Wortley Montagu, *Verses Addressed to the Imitator of Horace*, in which Pope was told :

— none thy crabbed numbers can endure,
Hard as thy heart, and as thy birth obscure.

Pope would not tolerate any of the three charges made against him. However, these charges were not the sole reason for Pope's satirisation of Hervey. Pope loathed the negative thinking of people like Hervey who had no fixed principles or loyalties. Pope was disgusted with the Satanic bend in Hervey's mind.

The poem is in the form of a conversation between the poet and Dr. Arbuthnot. At the opening of 'the portrait' Dr. Arbuthnot tends to dismiss Sporus as an insignificant creature, a "thing of silk" and "mere white curd of ass's milk" who over-reacts to situations. Pope might have been indebted to the fifteenth epigram of Ben Jonson, 'On Court-worm,' for the imagery in these lines. The epigram reads :

All men are worms : but this no man. In silk
'Twas brought to court first wrapt, and white as milk;

Where, afterwards, it grew a butterfly :
Which was a caterpillar. So't will die.

Ass's milk is the food of babies and invalids. Both Hervey and Pope were obliged to take this food by their physical condition. H.H. Erskine-Hill is of the opinion that "Something of Pope's hatred of his own invalid state and feeble constitution can be detected in these lines." Such a reading of the lines may be unwarranted although there are parts of the *Epistle* which abound in autobiographical details.

What is of greater significance is the animal imagery in the extract as in the entire poem. They are all connected in a kind of evolution, he points out. These images present animals, filth, disease, persecution and the virtuous man. The animal image yields the filth, because the animals mentioned are obnoxious creatures. The filth generates disease which turns into persecution, and in the face of persecution emerges in victory the virtuous man.

Mengel goes on to explain that to Pope poetasters like Hervey are men who "write and act without thinking, in automatic response to certain stimuli." Pope compares them to frogs that live on flies and spiders that live in their own filth. The result of such living is disease. Carrying their infections with them, they descend on Pope who is forced to slap them in self-defence. Hence his satire (the slap in self-defence), implies Pope, is justified, however harsh and topical it may be. Pope sees himself as the virtuous man who emerges victorious after the battle between the good and the evil. In the part that follows the portrait of Sporus, Pope presents himself as a righteous man.

Returning to the portrait of Sporus, we can see that Pope is not willing to dismiss his rival as easily as Dr. Arbuthnot is. This is because Pope is much more aware of the potential viciousness of Sporus than his friend is. Pope starts by calling Sporus a bug which buzzes around annoying both "the witty and the fair" as he is incapable of appreciating either wit or beauty. Unable to appreciate these qualities, he can make his presence felt only by 'stinging' the persons who do possess them. He is not merely an insect whose buzz and sting reveal his "florid impotence," but a person without any virtue whatsoever. The sheer emptiness of his soul is manifest in his "eternal smiles." Such a person is potentially Satan himself. Hence Pope calls him the toad "at the ear of Eve." Satan's attempt, by successfully tempting Eve, was to corrupt goodness. Sporus thus becomes "the incarnation of the desire to bring evil out of good" (Peter Dixon), the incarnation of Satan.

Satan tempted Eve in the guise of a serpent who pretended to be a well-wisher of mankind. He claimed to be offering man wisdom, whereas he was in fact corrupting his soul. He was at once the enemy and false friend of man. Sporus is none other than an incarnation of that Satan : "A cherub's face, a reptile all the rest."

It is this Satanic trait in the character of Sporus that is the target of Pope's attack. The trait is as dangerous as it is vicious. A combination of "the trifling head" and "the corrupted heart" is a serious threat to humanity. It can corrupt innocence and goodness by its affectations, because the innocent and the good will often fail to recognise the "venom" lying hidden in the "froth." This "amphibious" nature of Sporus consists in his pretension to goodness while he indulged in evil deeds.

Sporus is without a personality of his own. Hence he will keep 'see-sawing between that and this.'

> Now high, now low, now Master up, now Miss,
> And he himself one vile antithesis.

He is at once a servile flatterer and a scurrilous detractor. Plutarch defines the flatterer as a man who is "never consonant to himself, nor properly his own man...all his passions, his love and hatred, his joy and sorrow, are borrowed and counterfeit." Sporus is a counterfeit personality at its abysmal depth. Hence he becomes the "antithesis" to everything that is good.

Pope was constantly concerned with moral goodness. J Butt says that Pope composed the *Epistle to Dr. Arbuthnot* "in reply to the doctor's request...to continue his tirade against vice." His own moral character was the strong foundation on which Pope built up his satirical edifices. That is why he was able to attack boldly the vices he found in his society. Swift's view that much of Pope's satire is topical is true, but the topicality has not much detracted from its merit of universality. The universality is due to the fact that through the individuals, whom he attacks, Pope is attacking specific vices commonly found in human beings irrespective of time and place.

8

Romantic Poetry : Introduction

The Period

The period of Romantic poetry began in 1798 with the publication of *Lyrical Ballads*, a collection of poems composed by Wordsworth and Coleridge. The Preface to *Lyrical Ballads* denounced the poetic diction of the preceeding century and proposed to deal with materials from "common life" in "a selection of language really used by men." The poems in that volume not only marked a significant change in poetic diction, but showed a quite different attitude to poetry in general.

The cause of this attitudinal change may be traced to the socio-political situation of the period. The eighteenth century regarded society as a great constructive force which ideally holds all ranks of people together in mutually supporting harmony. But society, for the Romantics, had become an evil force — "a dark, repressive cloud, limiting action and obscuring perception" (Claire Lamont). Politically, the Romantic period coincided with the French Revolution. In its idealistic early stage, the Romantic movement, like the French Revolution, involved breaking out of the restrictive patterns of the past. The movement was also inspired by the revolution in America and the popular wars of independence in Poland, Spain and Greece. Philosophically, the Romantic movement was a reaction against the rationalism and scientism of the eighteenth century. Emotionally, it was an extreme assertion of the self. When the validity of reason as the only method of inquiry came to be questioned, the value of the individual's varied experiences obtained due importance. In addition to that was the sense of the infinite and the transcendental.

1832, generally taken as the end of the Romantic period, was the year in which the Reform Bill was passed in England. It marked the end of a phase of political agitations in the country and the beginning of a strong democracy.

Characteristics of Romantic Poetry

1. Innovation

In literature, breaking away from the past inevitably results in new forms. The Romantic poetry sought for and found new forms and style, without regard for classical precedent. For example, the serious or tragic treatment of lowly subjects in common language violated the basic neoclassic rule of decorum. Romantic poetry rendered "the charm of novelty to things of everyday."

2. The Poet's Isolation from Society

Rejecting society as an evil force which stunts its citizens, the Romantic poet became a solitary figure engaged in a quest. The quest is often long and sometimes very elusive. The rebel as the protagonist in many important Romantic works is an indication of the Romantic poet's isolation and personal quest. "The poet's isolated sensibility," as Stephen Spender says in his Preface to *A Choice of English Romantic Poetry*, "often takes an egotistic form which sets up tremendous claims." For example, Wordsworth demanded an intuitive understanding and oneness with nature (which was his quest); Shelley's claim that poets were the "unacknowledged legislators of mankind" is inextricable from his quest; and Keats sought to achieve complete self-realisation in a world created by the imagination. Furthermore, the whole eighteenth century demand for objectivity and rationality was denounced by the Romantic poets. Objectivity and rationality have little place in the world of the self.

3. Flight from the City

It was not merely the .society and its traditional attitudes that the Romantics denounced; the whole classical interest in cities was rejected. The classical literature had undoubtedly been metropolitan. It was associated with the Greek cities and with Rome. The English classicism was centred round London. The

Romantics rejected the culture of urbanisation and industrialisation and Shelley declared that "Hell is a city much like London."

4. Refuge in Nature

Fleeing from the increasing interest in urbanisation and industrialisation, the Romantics took refuge in the simple, primitive Nature. While their predecessors, the Augustans, looked on Nature as something incomplete and hence in need of man's help for its fulfillment, the Romantics regarded Nature as independent of man. It was man, according to these poets, who "needed the help of Nature to fulfil himself" (C. Lamont). Consequently, Nature became a persistent subject of Romantic poetry. It is generally described with accuracy and sensuous nuance. However, nature is not presented for its own sake; it becomes a stimulus for the poet to engage in meditation about some important human problem, to arouse his sense of sensuous beauty, and so on.

5. Withdrawal to Inner Experience

The Romantics took refuge in Nature because its vastness and mysteriousness provided them with infinite ways of exercising their imagination. The Romantic tendency is a tendency away from actuality. Speaking of this tendency, Lascelles Abercrombie says, "We see the spirit of the mind withdrawing more and more on the things it finds within itself." The Romantics withdraw from outer experience in order to concentrate on inner experience. It is a withdrawal from things perceived to things conceived.

Northorp Frye identifies two poles of mental activity. One is what he calls "sense;" *i.e.*, the recognition of what is presented by experience. The other pole is "the purely formalising or constructive aspect of the mind." In this attitude reality is something brought into being by the act of one's construction. While in pre-Romantic poetry there is a strong affinity with the attitude called sense, in Romantic poetry the emphasis is on the constructive powers of the mind. Frye goes to the extent of saying that the poetic technique of the Romantics is "akin to magic, which also aims at bringing spiritual forces into reality through concentration on a certain type of experience." It is also "akin to romance, with its efforts to maintain a self-consistent idealized world without the intrusion of realism or irony."

6. Importance of Imagination

The eighteenth century rationalism had relegated imagination to a secondary place. The poets of that century approved of 'fancy,' provided it was controlled by 'judgement.' For them the poet is an interpreter rather than creator, concerned with showing the attraction of what we already know.

According to the Romantics, imagination is the greatest faculty of a poet. Mind is the "central point and governing factor" and "the most vital activity of the mind is the imagination" (Maurice Bowra). Imagination sees things to which the ordinary intelligence is blind. Coleridge claims that imagination partakes of the creative ability of God. For Wordsworth, Keats and Shelley, imagination is concerned with a supernatural order.

7. Creation of Reality

The Romantic poet withdraws himself into his inner experience and with the help of his imagination gives shape to a new kind of reality. In the words of Stephen Spender, "At the back of the Romantic Movement is the idea that poetry creates its own kind of reality." Keats gives the impression that the world of the imagination is realer than the real world. In Shelley we find "a world of imagination transforming the real world by a kind of chemical action moving outwards from the imagination until finally it affects the shape of society." Wordsworth creates his kind of reality by a fusion of two shaping minds : one of Nature and the other of the poet. What this poetic creation of reality implies is a condition of affairs where poetry becomes the judge over life and society rather than *vice-versa*.

Spender further argues that the distinction between what is real and what is imagined is rather blurred in the world of Romantic poetry. It does not mean that the imagined world is the real world. "What the poets believe in, is the power of the creative imagination to invoke an ideal world : and in this ideal world, everything imagined is a means by which the poet lives his life into his poetry."

8. Romanticism is not opposed to Classicism

Although, Romanticism rebelled against the neo-classicism of the century that preceeded it, it is not the antithesis of classicism. Classicism is a holistic combination of the different elements of art. Romanticism is one element of art and hence of classicism. We can detect elements of Romanticism in classical works too. The difference is that while classicism holds the various elements of art in a balanced proportion, Romanticism has one element dominating its poetry. Abercrombie who upholds this view says, "The true antithesis of Romanticism is not classicism, but realism, which is another element of art."

9

Resolution and Independence

WILLIAM WORDSWORTH (1770-1850)

I

There was a roaring in the wind all night;
The rain came heavily and fell in floods :
But now the sun is rising calm and bright;
The birds are singing in the distant woods;
Over his own sweet voice the stock-dove broods;
The jay makes answer as the magpie chatters;
And all the air is filled with pleasant noise of waters.

II

All things that love the sun are out of doors;
The sky rejoices in the morning's birth;
The grass is bright with rain-drops; — on the moors
The hare is running races in her mirth;
And with her feet she from the plashy earth
Raises a mist, that, glittering in the sun,
Runs with her all the say, wherever she doth run.

III

I was a traveller then upon the moor,
I saw the hare that raced about with joy;
I heard the woods and distant waters roar;
Or heard them not, as happy as a boy :
The pleasant season did my heart employ :

My old remembrances went from me wholly;
And all the ways of men, so vain and melancholy.

IV

But, as it sometimes chanceth, from the might
Of joy in minds that can no further go,
As high as we have mounted in delight
In our dejection do we sink as low;
To me that did it happen so;
And fears and fancies thick upon me came;
Dim sadness — and blind thoughts, I knew not, nor
could name.

V

I heard the skylark warbling in the sky;
And I bethought me of the playful hare :
Even such a happy child of earth am I;
Even as these blissful creatures do I fare;
Far from the world I walk, and from all care;
But there may come another day to me —
Solitude, pain of heart, distress, and poverty.

VI

My whole life I have lived in pleasant thought,
As if life's business were a summer mood;
As if all needful things would come unsought
To genial faith, still rich in genial good;
But how can he expect that others should
Build for him, sow for him, and at his call
Love him, who for himself will take no heed at all?

VII

I thought of Chatterton, the marvellous boy,
The sleepless soul that perished in his pride;
Of him who walked in glory and in joy
Following his plough, along the mountainside :
By our own spirits are we deified :

We poets in our youth begin in gladness;
But thereof come in the end despondency and madness.

VIII

Now, whether it were by peculiar grace,
A leading from above, a something given,
Yet it befell, that, in this lonely place,
When I with these untoward thoughts had striven,
Beside a pool bare to the eye of heaven
I saw a man before me unawares :
The oldest man he seemed that ever wore grey hairs.

IX

As a huge stone is sometimes seen to lie
Couched on the bald top of an eminence;
Wonder to all who do the same espy,
By what means it could thither come, and whence :
So that it seems a thing endued with sense :
Like a sea-beast crawled forth, that on a shelf
Of rock or sand reposeth, there to sun itself.

X

Such seemed this man, not all alive nor dead,
Nor all asleep — in his extreme old age :
His body was bent double, feet and head
Coming together in life's pilgrimage;
As if some dire constraint of pain, or rage
Of sickness felt by him in times long past,
A more than human weight upon his frame had cast.

XI

Himself he propped, limbs, body, and pale face,
Upon a long grey staff of shaven wood :
And, still as I drew near with gentle pace,
Upon the margin of that moorish flood
Motionless as a cloud the old man stood,
That heareth not the loud winds when they call
And moveth all together, if it move at all.

XII

At length, himself unsettling, he the pond
Stirred with his staff, and fixedly did look
Upon the muddy water, which he conned,
As if he had been reading in a book :
And now a stranger's privilege I took;
And, drawing to his side, to him did say,
"This morning gives us promise of a glorious day."

XIII

A gentle answer did the old man make,
In courteous speech which forth he slowly drew :
And him with further words I thus bespake,
"What occupation do you there pursue?
This is a lonesome place for one like you."
Ere he replied, a flash of mild surprise
Broke from the sable orbs of his yet-vivid eyes.

XIV

His words came feebly, from a feeble chest,
But each in solemn order followed each,
With something of a lofty utterance drest —
Choice word and measured phrase, above the reach
Of ordinary men; a stately speech;
Such as grave livers do in Scotland use,
Religious men, who give to God and man their dues.

XV

He told, that to these waters he had come
To gather leeches, being old and poor :
Employment hazardous and wearisome!
And he had many hardships to endure :
From pond to pond he roamed, from moor to moor;
Housing, with God's good help, by choice or chance,
And in this way he gained an honest maintenance.

XVI

The old man still stood by my side;

But now his voice to me was like a stream
Scarce heard; nor word from word could I divide;
And the whole body of the man did seem
Like one whom I had met with in a dream;
Or like a man from some far region sent,
To give me human strength, by apt admonishment.

XVII

My former thoughts returned : the fear that kills;
And hope that is unwilling to be fed;
Cold, pain, and labour, and all fleshly ills;
And mighty poets in their misery dead.
— Perplexed, and longing to be comforted,
My question eagerly did I renew,
"How is it that you live, and what is it you do?"

XVIII

He with a smile did then his words repeat;
And said, that, gathering leeches, far and wide
He travelled stirring thus above his feet
The waters of the pools where they abide.
"Once I could meet with them on every side;
But they have dwindled long by slow decay;
Yet still I persevere, and find them where I may."

XIX

While he was talking thus, the lonely place,
The old man's shape, and speech — all troubled me :
In my mind's eye I seemed to see him pace
About the weary moors continually,
Wandering about alone and silently.
While I these thoughts within myself pursued.
He, having made a pause, the same discourse renewed.

XX

And soon with this he other matter blended,
Cheerfully uttered, with demeanour kind,
But stately in the main; and when he ended,

I could have laughed myself to scorn to find
In that decrepit man so firm a mind.
"God," said I, "be my help and stay secure :
I'll think of the leech-gatherer on the lonely moor!"

Critical Appreciation

The poem, "Resolution and Independence" (also known as 'The Leech-Gatherer') is about the poet and his life, rather, about human life in general, though the central figure in the poem is an old leech-gatherer whom Wordsworth and his sister, Dorothy, met on one of their walks. The poem makes no mention of Dorothy. Walking alone in an initial state of elation which soon gives way to apprehension and dejection, the poet comes across the old man whose appearance and words leave an indelible mark on him. The poem is a profound comment on human life, and in particular on the life of a poet.

The first two stanzas set the scene of the poem. The day has broken out with the "promise of a glorious day" after the storm and rain of the previous night. The morning presents a sun that is "rising calm and bright." It is a serene morning. The "roaring in the wind" and the rain which "fell in floods" have metamorphosed into the "sweet voice" of birds such as the stock-dove, jay and magpie and the "pleasant noise of waters" that fills the air. The magpie's chatter and the jay's answer to it implies the existence of "relationship and love" (Wordsworth's phrase in the Preface of 1802) in the nature around the poet. This hint about relationship and love and the open avowal of the mood of happiness in nature expresses the primal joy of existence itself.

The second stanza is at once an elaboration on the setting of the poem and a celebration of life. It speaks of fertility, birth and new life. The morning is a newly born infant over whose birth the sky rejoices. The grass is bright with the invigorating presence of rain drops on it. The hares are running about playfully on the moors. Their nimble feet raise a mist from the wet earth and it glitters in the sun. There is an immeasurable amount of gaiety in nature as "All things that love the sun are out of doors" and are in harmonious relationship with nature. In the words of Geoffrey Durrant, this stanza "insists on the fertility of nature, on the life which springs from sun and rain and earth, and is expressed in the animal vitality of the hare — a common symbol of fertility."

The scene that is set in these two stanzas illustrates the perfect harmony and vitality of nature. It leads the poet to consider his own condition, more as a poet and a human being than as an individual. The poet is distancing himself from this harmonious nature in order to consider "the ways of men" including him, and hence a change in the tense in the third stanza. The "now" of the first stanza becomes "then" in this stanza as the poet is caught by a mood of meditation about the fate of man. The poet is able to experience the harmony and joy of nature : his heart can be arrested by the sight of frolicking hare or the sound of the "distant waters." But he is also a victim of the usual human folly : vanity and melancholy. The poet is thinking of the "large gap between the harmonious life of nature and a man's own existence" (G. Durrant).

A man's capacity for joy is proportionate to his capacity for pain.

> As high as we have mounted in delight
> In our dejection do we sink as low; (stanza IV)

The poet is now overpowered by nameless "fears and fancies." It is the agony, the *angst* of existence itself. One may slide unexpectedly and without any reason from the mood of ecstasy to that of agony. Wordsworth wrote to Sara Hutchinson :

> (In this poem) I describe myself as having been exalted to the highest pitch of delight by the joyousness and beauty of nature; and then as depressed, even in the midst of these beautiful objects, to the lowest dejection and despair. A young poet in the midst of the happiness is described as overwhelmed by the thoughts of the miserable reverses which have befallen the happiest of all men, *viz.*, poets.

The poet is the happiest of all men because he enjoys a greater harmony with nature. In order to be one with nature like the "playful hare" or the warbling skylark, one needs to possess the primal innocence, the innocence of Adam and Eve before they came to know the distinction between good and evil. No man possesses that virtue. But the poet can on occasions rise to that state and then be "a happy child of earth." Those are the occasions when one becomes a "blissful creature" free from the cares of the world. These occasions are short-lived, however. A day may come when even these occasions are lost to the poet altogether, and his lot may be "solitude, pain of heart, distress, and poverty."

The poet is led to examine his own life which has been pleasant so far. Wordsworth regarded the pursuit of material progress as a serious obstacle to poetic commitment. In the sixth stanza he tells us of his belief that :

> all needful things would come unsought
> To genial faith, still rich in genial good.

It is the simple law of nature that goodness will have its reward. Yet, human as he is, the poet cannot but ask the question how he can expect others to care for him if he is unable to care for himself.

Having pondered on his own situation, the poet examines, in stanza VII, the lives of two other poets. One is Thomas Chatterton (1752-70) who was a very talented poet. At the age of 16 he published a passage written in archaic prose. It was followed by the 'Rowley' poems, purported to be the work of an imaginary fifteenth century poet, Thomas Rowley. Chatterton committed suicide, apparently reduced to despair by poverty. The other poet referred to by Wordsworth is Robert Burns (1759-96) who worked as a labourer and ploughman for the most part of his life. His poems were very popular. He remained poor till the time of his premature death, caused by rheumatic heart disease. Both these poets had their share of glory during their life-time. Yet both died in despair and sadness. Wordsworth generalises the fate of poets :

> We poets in our youth begin in gladness;
> But thereof come in the end despondency and madness.

Having thus reached the nadir of dejection, the poet is fortunate to get a "peculiar grace,/A leading from above, a something given." Like an apparition the leech-gatherer presents himself to the poet. The poet "does not so much meet the leech-gatherer as he becomes suddenly conscious of the old man before his eyes. It is as though the leech-gatherer is a visitant from another world, suddenly materializing before the gaze of the poet" (G. Durrant).

Stanzas IX, X and XI describe the leech-gatherer's appearance. Like a huge stone lying couched on top of a bald hill sits the old man beside a pool inducing a question in the mind of the observer :

By what means it could thither come, and whence :

The stone to which the old man is compared is itself compared to a sea-beast that crawls out of the sea in order to sun itself. Appearing neither fully alive, nor dead, nor all asleep, sat the old man with his body "bent double." He gives the impression of having suffered much "in times long past." He sits supporting himself against a staff. The poet compares him to a cloud which remains motionless even though the winds are blowing hard about it. If it moves at all it does so as one coherent mass.

Wordsworth himself had the following comment to make about these images.

> The stone is endowed with something of the power of life to approximate it to the sea-beast; and the sea-beast stripped of some of its vital qualities to assimilate it to the stone; which intermediate image is thus treated for the purpose of bringing the original image, that of the stone, to a nearer resemblance to the figure and condition of the aged man; who is divested of so much of the indications of life and motion as to bring him to the point where the two objects unite and coalesce in just comparison.

The importance of the images of the stone and the sea-beast thus seems to be that they unify the animate and the inanimate phenomena on the earth. The image of the cloud unifies the supernal phenomena with the earthly. Furthermore, since the "beast" belongs to the sea, the stone to the land and the cloud to the sky, these images can be said to be unifying the phenomena of the earth, water and air. In other words, in the vision of the poet, the old man becomes a symbol of the vast cosmos itself.

Stanza XII brings the poet down from his visionary elevation to the reality of the old man in front. The old man has moved a little and that is in order to stir the water in the pond with his staff. He then looks into the water "As if he had been reading in a book." Geoffrey Durrant argues that the old man staring into the water, suggests a diviner, a seer or a prophet. "And indeed that is what Wordsworth turns him into :" says Durrant, "the leech-gatherer is a sooth-sayer who reveals to the poet the truth about himself and his life."

The poet approaches the old man with the comment, "This morning gives us the promise of a glorious day." The morning has indeed given the poet that promise (stanzas I-III). But, sadly, that promise was short-lived; it gave way to the melancholy thoughts that rose strangely in the poet's mind (stanzas IV-VII). The sight of the old man, however, produced a vision and the poet perceived the unity of the cosmos (stanzas VIII-XI). Thus, the morning does indeed give a promise. The old man, who has now become a seer, is the cause of the present optimism.

The leech-gatherer tells the poet about his occupation. His words, though uttered feebly, have a peculiar solemnity; they are "above the reach/of ordinary men; a stately speech." He explains that he earns his livelihood by gathering leeches, a job that is both "hazardous and wearisome." He goes from pond to pond, from moor to moor, in search of leeches. Homeless though he may be, he is content with the shelter provided by the divine providence. He is happy that his occupation provides him with "an honest maintenance."

As the man speaks to the poet he once again becomes an apparition, an object in a vision. This time the vision is censorious of the poet. But the admonishment has an invigorating effect on him. It is going to give him "human strength," an attitude which will help him look at his life's woes differently.

Such an attitude cannot come upon a man all of a sudden. Psychological transitions are generally slow and painful. The poet returns to his former melancholy before he finally learns the lesson from the leech-gatherer. He experiences once again the *angst* of existence and a sense of hopelessness. Once again he is reminded of the tragic fate of great poets. He is tormented by the thought of man's situation in the world. Hence, his question, "How is it that you live, and what is it that you do?" asked even after the leech-gatherer's solemn utterance about his employment is not to be taken as a careless repetition of what the poet had already asked earlier. The question may be taken to mean : "What is the source of your endurance?" What the poet wonders is, how the leech-gatherer endures the burden of living when it is associated with acute consciousness of anxiety and pain. The old man repeats his story of perseverance. Endurance has no substitute, the old man teaches the poet. Endurance becomes a universal principle considering the poet's vision of the leech-gatherer as a symbol of the universe. In G. Durrant's words, "The old man ceases to be merely the leech-gatherer, and becomes instead an image of the human task, of commitment to consciousness, to the endless search for what is to be found, no matter what pain may be involved, or what the price to be paid."

10

Ode To The West Wind

PERCY BYSSHE SHELLEY (1792-1822)

I

O wild West Wind, thou breath of Autumn's being,
Thou, from whose unseen presence the leaves dead
Are driven, like ghosts from an enchanter fleeing.

Yellow, and black, and pale, and hectic red,
Pestilence-stricken multitudes : O thou
Who chariotest to their dark wintry bed

The winged seeds, where they lie cold and low,
Each like a corpse within its grave, until
Thine azure sister of the Spring shall blow

Her clarion o'er the dreaming earth, and fill
(Driving sweet buds like flocks to feed in air)
With living hues and odours, plain and hill

Wild Spirit, which art moving everywhere;
Destroyer and preserver; hear, oh, hear!

II

Thou on whose stream, 'mid the steep sky's commotion
Loose clouds like earth's decaying leaves are shed,
Shook from the tangled boughs of Heaven and Ocean,

Angels of rain and lightning : they are spread
On the blue surface of thine airy surge,
Like the bright hair uplifted from the head

Of some fierce Maenad, even from the dim verge
Of the horizon to the zenith's height,
The locks of the approaching storm, Thou dirge.

Of the dying year, to which this closing night
Will be the dome of a vast sepulchre,
Vaulted with all thy congregated might

Of vapours, from whose solid atmosphere
Black rain, and fire, and hail, will burst : oh, hear!

III

Thou who didst waken from his summer dreams
The blue Mediterranean, where he lay,
Lulled by the coil of his crystalline streams,

Beside a pumice isle in Baiae's bay,
And saw in sleep old palaces and towers
Quivering within the wave's intenser day,

All overgrown with azure moss and flowers
So sweet, the sense faints picturing them; Thou
For whose path the Atlantic's level powers

Cleave themselves into chasms, while far below
The sea-blooms and the oozy woods which wear
The sapless foliage of the ocean, know

Thy voice, and suddenly grow gray with fear,
And tremble and despoil themselves : oh, hear!

IV

If I were a dead leaf thou mightest bear;
If I were a swift cloud to fly with thee;
A wave to pant beneath thy power, and share

The impulse of thy strength, only less free
Than thou, O uncontrollable; If even
I were as in my boyhood, and could be

The comrade of thy wanderings over Heaven,
As then, when to outstrip thy skiey speed,
Scarce seemed a vision, I would ne'er have striven

As thus with thee in prayer in my sore need.
Oh, lift me as a wave, a leaf, a cloud!
I fall upon the thorns of life! I bleed!

A heavy weight of hours has chained and bowed
One too, like thee : tameless, and swift, and proud.

V

Make me thy lyre, even as the forest is :
What if my leaves are falling like its own!
The tumult of thy mighty harmonies

Will take from both a deep, autumnal tone,
Sweet though in sadness. Be thou, spirit fierce,
My spirit; Be thou me, impetuous one!

Drive my dead thoughts over the universe
Like withered leaves to quicken a new birth!
And, by the incantation of this verse,

Scatter, as from an unextinguished hearth
Ashes and sparks, my words among mankind!
Be through my lips to unawakened earth

The trumpet of a prophecy; O, Wind,
If winter comes, can Spring be far behind?

Critical appreciation

The 'Ode to the West Wind' was composed in the autumn of 1819 when Shelley was in Florence. According to Shelley, the poem "was conceived and chiefly written in a wood that skirts the Arno, near Florence, and on a day when the tempestuous wind, whose temperature is at once mild and animating, was collecting the vapours which pour down the autumnal rains."

The West Wind is to the poet not only a source of poetic inspiration but also a 'spirit,' a supernatural power. Frederick A Pottle points out that the "breath" ('spiritus') which Shelley invokes "was to him as real and as awful as the Holy Ghost was to Milton." Angela Leighton argues that the Ode "is an invocation of that Power which is the source of all activity, political as well as literary. According to A.E. Dyson and J. Lovelock, Shelley calls on the wind "as if it were some great Being, some Spirit from above."

It is because the West Wind is seen by the poet as something much more than a wind that there is a tone of prayer in the first three stanzas, each of which ends with the plea, "oh, hear!" However, as Timothy Webb suggests, the West Wind is not "a personal deity" to Shelley, but "an anonymous and unknown power." In spite of his arguments for the 'necessity of atheism' and all his spirit of rebellion against the God of Christianity, Shelley was a passionately religious person. He believed that there is a spirit in Nature, a spirit which constantly strives to penetrate and transform the material world. Shelley perceives that spirit in the West Wind.

In stanza I the West Wind is both "Destroyer and preserver." The stanza, like the others in the poem, is in the form of a sonnet, with four tercets and a couplet. The first two tercets of stanza I portray the destructive power of the West Wind while the next two are about its complementary powers and the last couplet synthesises both these aspects.

Autumn is the season that preceedes winter which is the season of death or of inertness as implied in the last lines of the Ode as well as in the phrase "dark wintry bed" in stanza I. Metaphorically autumn is the period of decline in the life of any organism after it has reached maturity. The West Wind is addressed as the breath of that period; it is the spirit of biological degeneration. The first part of stanza I is full of images of sickness and death. The leaves are dead and their movement in the wind is, not surprisingly, ghostly. The colours associated with "Pestilence-stricken multitudes" are colours of sickness and death. Dyson and Lovelock view "Yellow, and black, and pale" as colours of "jaundice and death," while "hectic red" adds "hints of haste and fever."

The "wintry bed" mentioned at the end of the first part of this stanza has two connotations; it is a deathbed, and it is also a bed in the soil from which new life will be generated. Thus the phrase serves to unite the two themes of death and rebirth in the stanza. The "wintry bed" is "dark" (hence, associated with death), but it is also the place to which the seeds impregnated with new life are carried and planted by the wind. The planting of the seed is envisaged by the poet as burial because each seed will lie in the bed "like a corpse within its grave." These seeds will sprout in the spring season, when the "azure sister" of the West Wind will blow her "clarion." The clarion call of the spring wind is reminiscent of the angel's trumpet call on the Day of the Judgement : "...the trumpet will sound, and the dead will be raised..." (1. Corinthians 15 : 52).

As pointed out by Dyson and Lovelock, the autumn destroyer and the "azure sister of the Spring" are the same wind which manifests itself in different seasons and different moods. The wind which is both "Destroyer and preserver" moves everywhere and thus its spirit is universal; it animates the whole universe. But it is not a god. "The wind is not likened to a god," says Dyson and Lovelock, "but *felt* as a god."

While the first stanza describes the creative and destructive powers of the wind on the land, the second stanza directs our attention to the effects of the wind in the sky or in the air. The wind now exerts its force on the clouds.

According to Desmond King—Hele's interpretation, the second stanza presents "a fine cloudscape, composed of two quite different types of cloud, fractostratus and cirrus." The fractostratus clouds are harbingers of rain and appear low in the west as jagged and detached clouds, approaching fast in the rising wind. The cirrus stretches from the horizon, which is dim because it is obscured by the fractostratus, to the zenith. King-Hele further points out that the simile of the Maenad is apt as "Maenads had the odd habit of rushing around with hair streaming." The word 'cirrus' literally means 'a lock of hair.'

Maenads were female members of the orgiastic cult of Dionysius. The cirrus clouds stretching from the horizon to the zenith look like the hair of a Maenad blown forward from her head by the wind. These clouds are "the locks of the approaching storm" because spreading cirrus clouds often herald a depression.

The West Wind, which was addressed by the poet as the spirit of autumn in stanza I, now becomes the "dirge/of the dying year." The enveloping darkness of the cloudy night will be the dome of the vast tomb in which the dying year will be buried. The clouds which reveal the might of the West Wind will form the vault of this tomb. From this "solid" vault will fall on the earth "Black rain, and fire, and hail."

The first stanza presented the wind as both destroyer and preserver. The seeds buried by the west wind will be regenerated by the same wind later. The second stanza too speaks of a burial, that of the dying year. The poet, however, mentions nothing of the new year that will be born. Instead he concentrates on the terrifying effects of the wind on the clouds which culminate in torrential rain accompanied with lightning and hailstorm.

The tone mellows in the next stanza which speaks of the action of the wind on the ocean. The wind wakes up the Mediterranean from its "summer dreams." However, until it was woken up by the wind, the Mediterranean was lying "lulled to sleep by the sound of streams flowing into it." The streams "produce the effect of currents observed on the surface as coils, gently binding as well as lulling the recumbent inland sea" (Patrick Swinden).

The particular part of the Mediterranean described by Shelley is the Bay of Baiae which was a fashionable resort of the Romans in the ancient times. There were majestic palaces and towers built there by the Roman rulers. But they were destroyed by an eruption of a volcano, the Vesuvius. Shelley sailed on the Bay of Baiae in Dec 1818 during his stay at Naples. He refers in a letter to "the ruins of its antique grandeur standing like rocks in the transparent sea under our boat.... The sea ... was so translucent that you could see the hollow caverns clothed with glaucous sea-moss, and the leaves and branches of those delicate weeds that pave the unequal bottom of the water."

In the third stanza of the Ode Shelley imagines the ancient submerged palaces and towers to be covered with moss and sea-weeds, which are the things now visible at the bottom of the "translucent" sea. The sight is so beautiful that the very visualisation of it ("picturing them") is enough to make the poet's sense faint.

The effect of the West Wind on the Mediterranean seems to be merely to wake up the ocean from its complacent sleep and to reveal to us the fascinating beauty submerged in its waters. But in the second half of the stanza the wind's action on another ocean, the Atlantic, becomes more energetic and even fierce. The Atlantic, responding to the powers of the wind, cleaves itself into chasms. The power of the wind makes furrows on the surface of the ocean. The vegetation at the bottom of the sea recognizes the power of the wind and not only "grow gray with fear" but "tremble and despoil themselves."

In a note Shelley wrote : "The vegetation at the bottom of the sea, of rivers, and of lakes, sympathises with that of the land in the change of seasons, and is consequently influenced by the winds which announce it." Shelley seems to be suggesting that all phenomena, whether on the land, in the sky or under the ocean, are influenced by the power of the west wind, which is a symbol of the degenerative and regenerative spirit in nature.

Having described the power of the wind on the natural phenomena, the poet now turns to his self. He wishes he were "a dead leaf," "a swift cloud," or "a wave" so that he too could experience the destructive and creative power of the wind, and thus share the impulse of its strength.

For a moment Shelley dwells upon the days of his boyhood when he "could be/The comrade of thy (the wind's) wanderings over heaven." He was then able to participate in the mighty power of the nature's spirit. Not able to participate in it, is to be alienated from the very essence of life. Shelley believed that nature is as much alive as man is and has a soul too. Everything on the earth is directed by this soul. Shelley says directly that once he too was like this soul symbolized by the West Wind : "tameless, and swift, and proud." However, at the present moment, he feels that he has been "chained and bowed" by "A heavy weight of hours."

In the words of Dyson and Lovelock, "this poem, while not being in any way Christian, comes close to Christianity in its pervasive apprehension of ambivalent relationships with the power flowing through creation — at one with it in desire, but exiled in fact." In Shelley's poems, in general we can detect an undertone of sadness which seems to arise from his relation that man is a great spirit which is in exile from the greater and freer worlds to which he really belongs. Hence the earnest prayer to the spirit of the West Wind to "lift me as a wave, a leaf, a cloud!" In effect, the poet is praying to the wind to enable him to rise above the bondages of life and to be vital part of the soul of nature.

The line, "I fall upon the thorns of life! I bleed!" has been seen as a blemish on the poem by many critics because, as Swinden says, it is "totally quite out of key with the poem." The poem is about the great moulding power of nature. The poet is praying to it too, while he is describing its power. But the tone is never sentimental and self-pitying as in the line in question. Nevertheless, the line serves to underscore the present impotent condition of the poet.

The poem began with a description of the onslaught of the wind upon such passive, will-less attributes of nature as the leaves and the seeds. In the second stanza, the wind becomes a transformer : it transforms the clouds into furious rains. Eventually the Wind is able to rouse up "the Atlantic's level powers" into action; it is no more the wind acting on passive objects. The poet too wants to be roused up into action.

The poet has understood that he cannot compete with the wind any more (although he was once like the wind : "tameless, and swift, and proud") because he remains chained to the earth by his personal sorrows. He is unable to submit himself to the power of the wind totally, because ideally he is a part of it, not separate element which needs submission. Hence, all that the poet can now pray for is to be made an instrument of the wind. He prays that he be made a lyre, like the forest, on which the wind will play. The poet hopes to reveal to the world "the tumult" of the wind's "mighty harmonies."

The poet is aware of himself as a shattered man even in this part of the poem. He grieves that he has reached the autumn of his life : "What if leaves are falling." He acknowledges his sadness. But he knows that sadness can produce "sweet" music. In 'To a Skylark' Shelley wrote the oft-quoted line :

"Our sweetest songs are those that tell of saddest thought." When Shelley prays to the wind to be himself ("Be thou me, impetuous one!") he is asking for the power to rise out of his present impotent state, out of despair, not out of sorrow. He is asking for regeneration.

The poem has spoken of the regenerative power of the wind. The poet himself now is in need of "a new birth." He prays to the wind to drive "his dead thoughts," as it has driven the leaves and the seeds, so that they will receive a new life. Like the clarion call of the wind which will rouse up the seeds to new life, the poet wants to be a prophetic voice to "unawakened earth." It is not only the poet who is in need of renewed life; the world stands in need of change. That the poet's message will be as revolutionary as the wind's effect has been tumultuous is implied in the phrase "ashes and sparks." The poet wants to share in the moulding power of the wind so that he can be the revolutionary, the prophet, who will rouse up the world from its wintry stupour to regenerated vitality.

The ode is a powerful expression of the theme of destruction and creation, death and rebirth. It is full of a mighty energy which can transform despair' and suffering into hope and endurance. The rhythm of the ode is in harmony with this mighty energy. This energy reveals Shelley's boldness "to welcome autumnal sadness and wintry bareness, finding in the wild wind which sweeps the forest leaves away an exultant harbinger of the awakening year" (E. Dowden).

11

Ode To A Nightingale

JOHN KEATS (1795-1821)

1

My heart aches, and a drowsy numbness pains
  My sense, as though of hemlock I had drunk,
Or emptied some dull opiate to the drains
  One minute past, and Lethe-wards had sunk :
'Tis not through envy of thy happy lot,
  But being too happy in thine happiness, —
    That thou, light-winged Dryad of the trees,
      In some melodious plot
Of beechen green, and shadows numberless,
      Singest of summer in full-throated ease.

2

O for a draught of vintage; that hath been
  Cool'd a long age in the deep-delved earth,
Tasting of flora and the country green,
  dance, and Provencal song, and sun-burnt mirth!
O, for a beaker full of the warm South,
  Full of the true, the blushful Hippocrene,
    With beaded bubbles winking at the brim,
      And purple-stained mouth;
That I might drink, and leave the world unseen,
      And with thee fade away into the forest dim.

3

Fade far away, dissolve, and quite forget

What thou among the leaves hast never known,
The weariness, the fever, and the fret
Here, where men sit and hear each other groan;
Where palsy shakes a few, sad, last grey hairs,
Where youth grows pale, and spectre-thin, and dies;
Where but to think is to be full of sorrow
And leaden-eyed despairs;
Where beauty cannot keep her lustrous eyes,
Or new love pine at them beyond tomorrow.

4

Away! away! for I will fly to thee,
Not charioted by Bacchus and his pards,
But on the viewless wings of Poesy,
Though the dull brain perplexes and retards!
Already with thee! tender is the night;
And haply the Queen Moon is on her throne,
Cluster'd around by all her starry Fays;
But here there is no light,
Save what from heaven is with the breezes blown
Through verdurous glooms and winding mossy ways.

5

I cannot see what flowers are at my feet,
Nor what soft incense hangs upon the boughs,
But, in embalmed darkness, guess each sweet
Wherewith the seasonable month endows
The grass, the thicket, and the fruit-tree wild;
White hawthorn, and the pastoral eglantine
Fast-fading violets covered up in leaves;
And mid-May's eldest child
The coming musk-rose, full of dewy wine,
The murmurous haunt of flies on summer eves.

6

Darkling I listen; and, for many a time
I have been half in love with easeful Death,
Call'd him soft names in many amused rhyme,

To take into the air my quiet breath;
Now more than ever seems it rich to die,
To cease upon the midnight with no pain,
While thou art pouring forth thy soul abroad
In such ecstasy!
Still wouldst thou sing, and I have ears in vain —
To thy high requiem become a sod.

7

Thou wast not born for death, Immortal Bird!
No hungry generations tread thee down;
The voice I hear this passing night was heard
In ancient days by emperor and clown;
Perhaps the self-same song that found a path
Through the sad heart of Ruth, when, sick for home,
She stood in tears amid the alien corn;
The same that oft-times hath
Charm'd magic casements, opening on the foam
Of perilous seas, in faery lands forlorn.

8

Forlorn! the very word is like a bell
To toll me back from thee to my sole self!
Adieu! the fancy cannot cheat so well
As she is famed to do, deceiving elf.
Adieu! adieu! thy plaintive anthem fades
Past the near meadows, over the still stream,
Up the hill-side and now 'tis buried deep
In the next valley-glades :
Was it a vision, or a waking dream?
Fled is that music : — do I wake or sleep?

Critical appreciation

All the great odes of Keats written in the spring of 1819 have a basic theme : the conflict between man's painful consciousness of transience and his intuitive perceptions of permanence. Consciousness or what Keats calls "the thinking principle" is self-awareness and awareness of the world that surrounds, nurtures and conditions the self (Morris Dickstein, *Keats and His Poetry : A Study in Development*). Hence consciousness is inevitably associated with the human and mutable, while man's intuition lets him perceive the immortal and essential. Such an intuitive perception may be brief and fleeting. It is precisely this nature of the intuitive perception that poses a problem for Keats. He knows that human as we are, we cannot perpetualise these moments of intuitive perception, let alone the values they present. On the other hand, Keats is also aware of the validity of consciousness in human existence; without consciousness we would not be in vital touch with the reality around us. Sheer flight from consciousness would be an act of escapism. Not only the odes, but most of Keats, poetry deals with this dilemma. Obviously much of what his poetry states has something to do with both an opposition and a fusion of these two elements : the painful consciousness and the blissful intuition. The theme of the 'ode to a Nightingale' is not different either.

The 'ode to a Nightingale' was composed in a single morning. Keats was residing in the house of Charles Brown at that time. "In the spring of 1819," writes Brown, "a nightingale had built her nest near my house. Keats felt a tranquil and continual joy in her song; and one morning he took his chair from the breakfast-table to the grass-plot under a plum-tree, where he sat for two or three hours." The ode was written in those two or three hours, according to Brown.

The movement of the poem, as argued by Earl R. Wasserman (*The Finer Tone*), is from an intuitive perception of the immortal and immutable reality to the painful consciousness of the transient reality around. It is a downward movement. That accounts for the presence of many irreconcilables in thé ode.

Before the poem opens, the poet has had an ecstatic experience. The "tranquil and continual joy" that Keats experienced was a result of his absorption into the transcendental reality by means of the nightingale's song. But now he is returning to his self; hence the dark tone of intense pain in the opening lines. This is made clear when the poet asserts that his heartache is due not to envy in the bird's "happy lot," but to his having been "too happy in thy happiness." Return to the mutable reality from the experience of immutable essence is a process of disintegration which the poet's self would tend to resist, though the resistance is futile as the return is inevitable. The "drowsy numbness" that pains the poet's "sense" (*i.e.*, mind and feeling) is caused by this semi-conscious resistance to an inevitable process.

According to Keats, the highest joy that one can achieve is to lose one's consciousness and be assimilated blissfully into immutable essence. The nightingale is experiencing that bliss. It has become one with nature, or the essence of nature. Keats calls it "Dryad," a nymph which lives in the woods, rather a nymph whose life is that of the tree she inhabits. The poet too has had an empathic relationship with the bird, and through it, with essence. However, he is now regressing from blissful unconsciousness to painful consciousness, and the state of stupour described in the first four lines of the poem may be said to be the intervening state between the above-mentioned states.

The nightingale's song is of summer while the ode is set in "mid-May" (stanza V). Summer is the period in the temporal world when the inner essence of nature comes to fruition and becomes manifest (Wasserman). The nightingale is singing of that fullness as it is partaking of that fullness.

The first stanza presents a contrast between the poet and the bird. The languid movement of the first half of the stanza indicates the poet's condition while the easy flow of the second half symbolizes the bird's blissful singing. The contrast deepens in the succeeding stanzas as the poet seeks means of escape from his mental agony.

The first remedy that the poet proposes is wine. Wine may provide some sort of substitute for the bliss which the nightingale's song provided earlier. That the poet is seeking to transcend his self through intoxication is implied by the attributes attached to wine by the poet. The wine has been

> Cool'd a long age in the deep-delved earth,
> Tasting of flora and the country green,
>
> Dance, And Provencal song, and sunburnt mirth!

To the wine are attributed the rejuvenating powers of the earth and of nature as well as the revitalizing potentiality of human culture. That the wine can provide inspiration is suggested by the mention of the Hippocrene, which is a fountain on Mount Helicon in Greece, held sacred to the Muses and regarded as the source of poetic inspiration.

Poetry is the next remedy proposed by the poet for his present condition. The belief that the Hippocrene was created by Pegasus, the winged horse of Greek mythology, may be regarded as a pointer to "the viewless wings of Poesy" Keats mentions in stanza IV. But before coming to the explicit mention of poetry as a means of escape from consciousness, the poet once again asserts his faith, false though it turns out to be, in the redeeming power of wine :

> That I might drink, and leave the world unseen,
> And with thee fade away into the forest dim :

Stanzas II and III present the same contrast which the two halves of stanza I showed us : between the bird's and the poet's states. The romantic and pastoral ideal portrayed in stanza II is properly the bird's realm to which the poet is aspiring through the medium of intoxication. But the world of painful reality depicted in stanza III is where the poet actually finds himself. It is a world of feverish activity and weariness, complaints and despairs, helplessness and premature death. It is a world of terrible transience.

> Where beauty cannot keep her lustrous eyes,
> Or new love pine at them beyond tomorrow.

In the 'Ode on a Grecian Urn,' Keats speaks of a world of permanence where music remains ever-sweet and love remains ever-passionate. Here in stanza III of the nightingale ode we have a contrary world.

It has been pointed out by many critics that the line, "Where Youth grows pale, and spectre-thin, and dies;" has an implicit reference to Tom, Keats' brother, who died seven months before the composition of the 'Ode to a Nightingale.' Keats read King Lear on Oct. 4, 1818, a few weeks before Tom's death. He underlined the words "poor Tom" in Edgar's sentence : "The foul fiend haunts poor Tom in the voice of a nightingale." Hence, the argument that Keats had Tom in mind when he wrote the above-quoted line is not without relevance. However, the emphasis of the third stanza is on the tragic mutability of this world as contrasted with the nightingale's world of unalloyed bliss. The nightingale is outside the context of physical nature : it "among the leaves hast never known" the agonies of this world. The poet belongs, however, to the physical world, and even wine cannot provide him with the required release from it.

The next contrast between the poet and the bird reveals itself in stanzas IV and V. Stanza II ended with a simple expression of the poet's desire to "fade away" with the nightingale. Stanza IV opens with a passionate resolution to fly to the bird. In the phrases of Wasserman, "the optative exclamation" of stanza II gives was to the "passionate power of the resolute." Having realized that wine will only bring a very brief solace from the fever and fret of this world, the poet is now determined to reach the nightingale's bliss

> Not charioted by Bacchus and his pards,
> But on the viewless wings of Poesy,

because ideal poetry is able to penetrate into the essence of things.

At this stage of the poem, when the poet proposes to take recourse to poetry in order to achieve union with the world of essence, the nightingale is already in that world. Everything has become transparent to the bird in the light of "the Queen-Moon" and her attendants, the "starry Fays." The night or the darkness has become tender and the nightingale is now participating in the essence of reality by virtue of its having penetrated through the darkness that surrounds the essence.

The line "Already with thee! Tender is the night" has been interpreted by many critics like W.J. Bate and M.R. Ridley as an indication of the poet's brief union with the bird. It is this union, argue some critics, that enables the poet in stanza V to have a deeper perception into the nature around him. He is able to see the blessings of spring on "The grass, the thicket, and the fruit-tree wild;" on the hawthorn, the eglantine and musk-rose. Geoffrey Hartman regards this stanza as "the middle-ground of imaginative activity, not reaching to vision, not falling into blankness." Morris Dickstein calls this middle-ground "a lower paradise."

Wasserman denounces the above interpretation of the line as it can "lead only to inconsistencies, if not to nonsense". He seems to be right when we look at the last three lines of the stanza. The nightingale has reached the milieu which offers transparency into the mystery of nature. But for the poet "here there is no light," except the gentle flicker blown from heaven by the "breezes" through "verdurous glooms" and "mossy ways." This flicker does not enable the poet to see anything, not even the flowers at his feet. Whatever he describes in stanza V are what he "guesses."

In one of the transcripts (E) of the ode the line did not contain an exclamation mark. It read :

> Already with thee tender is the night:

The exclamation marks seems to have been added, contends Wasserman, to transfer the emphasis from "with," where the meter places it. If that is the case the line should mean that the night is tender with the nightingale. The same night leaves the poet in blinding darkness. The contrast in these two stanzas in between the bird which has reached the luminous milieu and the poet who remains in "embalmed darkness." The bird has penetrated into the mystery of life, while the poet has only been given flickers of guesses.

Stanzas VI and VII present the final contrast between the nightingale and the poet. The bird now becomes immortal while the poet, agonizingly conscious of the transience of his world, longs for the ultimate termination of transience : death. Keats admits that he has been "half in live with easeful Death" many a time. He wrote to Charles Brown on Sept. 30, 1820 :

> I wish for death every day and night... and then I wish it away, for death would destroy even those pains which are better than nothing. Land and sea, weakness and decline, are great separators, but death is the great divorcer for ever.

In 'Why Did I Laugh Tonight?' he wrote :

> Verse, fame, and beauty are intense indeed,
> But death intenser — Death is life's high mead.

Obviously, Keats regarded physical death as a means of reaching the highest experience man can : union with essence. Hence, Graham Hough's interpretation of the opening lines of stanza VI as a kind of Freudian death-wish, *i.e.*, "the desire of the cell to resist the encroachments of the outside experience, to remain enclosed in its own kind of contentment" (*The Romantic Poets*), may not be quite right. The death spoken of in stanza VI is actual physical death, and that is the poet's third proposal as a remedy for his present mental condition. This proposal too will turn out to be as futile as the other two.

Morris Dickstein regards stanza VI of the nightingale ode as "the most significant moment in Keats's poetry, and one of the most important in all Romantic literature." He explains :

> It is the culminating moment of Keats's lifelong struggle against consciousness, his quest for self-annihilation made all the more complicated by his strong commitment to 'the thinking principle' and to the painful extension of that desire for self-annihilation is the desire for death, the wish to be wholly free of the burdens of selfhood, a longing to which so many of the Romantics were willing prey.

With the third proposal, that of death, the poet and the bird have moved to opposite poles. The nightingale is addressed as "immortal bird" while the poet is "a sod," a corpse for which the nightingale is now singing a "high requiem." This is the climax of the series of contrasts we have been following in the poem.

At first the bird's blissful selflessness was contrasted with the poet's painful descent into consciousness of self and its surroundings from the selfless ecstasy which he had shared with the bird. The poet's proposal of wine presented the second contrast : an ideal physical setting contrasted with the agonies of actual existence. The third contrast shifted the focus from the physical to the perceptive : the nightingale penetrated into the dark mystery of life and nature, while the poet remained in darkness. The last contrast makes a spirit of the nightingale while the poet himself is the most material of matter : "a sod."

The nightingale's immortality has been interpreted variously. W.J. Bate says that the immortality "is that of the species." Viewed that way, man is immortal too as the human species will continue from generation to generation. Dickstein suggests that what is immortal is the nightingale's song which is "not only identical in all periods of history but also, unlike the poet, self-less." Generations of men have listened to the nightingale's song, as suggested in stanza VII, and they have all been fascinated by the "self-sameness" or lack of individual identity of that song. In addition to the 'identity-less-ness' of the song, the nightingale's lack of awareness and imagination is what makes the song immortal, according to Aileen Ward (*John Keats : The Making of a Poet*). Wasserman argues that the nightingale in the ode is immortal because it is a symbolic bird which has risen out of mortality, by virtue of the attributes given to it in the poem, and has come into the presence of the immortal essence.

Whatever the nature of the nightingale's immortality, it has had the ability to capture the attention of man, in history, legend and romance. Man has always been able to establish an enriching relationship with the nightingale's song. Emperors as well as clowns have listened to it. Ruth is a character from a Biblical legend. She was destined to live as a widow in Bethlehem, far away from the land of her own people, the Moabites. However, she was blessed with a happy family life when Boaz, a man of Bethlehem, married her. Her tale is one of endurance and its reward. The "charm'd magic casements" gives us a similar picture of young maidens awaiting their lovers to come and rescue them from the tedium of life in the castle. This is a picture taken from medieval romances. In short, generations of people have listened to the nightingale's song and found solace in it. However painful the human condition is, man still possesses the capacity to respond to immortal beauty, and thus to establish a communion with the immutable order of the world of essence.

Is it this realisation that transports the poet suddenly from the visionary plane to the plane of his naked self in stanza VIII? The stanza begins with the word "Forlorn!," a word which has been discussed much by critics. Aileen Ward is of the opinion that the word "suggests in the faintest of overtones" that Keats' quest to project himself into an essence outside him "may prove an illusion in the end." The word is the result of the implicit but growing disenchantment of the poet with the nightingale, according to Dickstein. He says that what the nightingale presented was a mere 'dream-world,' and hence Keats calls it "deceiving elf" in the last stanza. For Graham Hough the word reveals the contradiction between the poet who creates an ideal world and the man who suffers in the actual world. The last stanza is "something of an anticlimax" in the view of Ridley because "the poetic ecstasy is over and the poet comes back wearily to reality" (*Keats' Craftsmanship*).

Even Wasserman, to whom the conclusive word has been given in many places in this essay, seems to admit the ambivalence of the last stanza. It is undeniable that the poet's vision has ended and his return to his self is now complete. After a passionate attempt to penetrate into the darkness, the mystery of life, the poet finds himself in daylight; but the light gives no insight into the mystery. The nightingale has been assimilated into that dark mystery. What about the poet? His final realisation is what is ambivalent according to Wasserman. Was the poet's experience indeed a vision or a mere dream? If it was a vision, answers Wasserman, the poet has seen momentarily into the mystery of life. If it was only a dream, then we ought to conclude that the very existence of man is a transitory moment of dark ignorance.

12

Victorian Poetry : Introduction

The Period

The Victorian age witnessed rapid scientific progress. James Watt's steam engine revolutionized the industries. Passenger railways (the first of which was opened in 1830) and the electric telegraph (which came into existence in 1835) made communication faster and more convenient. The various factories were owned by a small class of capitalists whose sole aim was to amass great fortunes for themselves. This led to the creation of two classes of people in England : the wealthy industrialists and the poor working class. She working class people were ill-treated in the factories. The worked for fifteen to eighteen hours a day for scandalously low wages. Women and children were employed in large numbers in the factories.

The economic impact aside, science also affected people's attitudes to religious faith and human relationships. Although Charles Darwin's *Origin of Species* appeared only in 1859 to shake the very foundations of people's religious faith, skepticism had already taken root at least in a section of the people. Calling it "the Mechanical Age," Thomas Carlyle wrote in 1829 about the England of the period : "Men are grown mechanical in head and heart, as well as in hand" ('Signs of the Times'). A "mechanical" approach to relationships, attachments, and opinions, coupled with increasing rationalism created a conflict between faith and doubt, tradition and innovation, conservatism and reform.

The intellectuals reacted differently to these conflicts. Some, like John Henry Newman, adhered even more to the Church and led the Oxford Movement which, along with what Newman

Called the 'Second Spring' of the English Roman Catholic Church, "offered a kind of certainty and an assertion of tradition to a nation increasingly beset withy uncertainty and the consequence of progressive change" (Andrew Sanders). Some, like Arthur Hugh Clough, became rudderless, lost their faith and turned agnostic. Some, like Matthew Arnold, substituted morality for God. Most Victorian intellectuals, argue N.P. Messenger and J.R. Watson, remained amused and skeptical or disturbed and directionless :

> Wandering between two worlds, one dead,
> The other powerless to be born.
>
> (Arnold, 'Stanzas from the Grande Chartreuse')

The successful Victorian man was the industrialist, the capitalist, who remained serious, comfortable and prosperous. They had religious faith too. It is they, along with the progressive benefits and ideas advanced by science, who provided stability to the Victorian society. Moreover, there was no great political upheaval during the period. After 1815, England was involved in no major war for a century. Even the Napoleonic Wars which lasted until 1815 had only helped to increase enormously the volume of English trade.

Poetry of the Period

The Victorian poetry, which marks the transition from the Romantic to the Modern, attempted with fair success in experimentation with respect to style and subject matter. One of the most significant advances in the history of English poetry is the kind of dramatic monologues written during this period, especially the kind written by Robert Browning (see 'My Last Duchess' and the critical notes to it). In the words of Joseph Bristow, these monologues "indicate how language speaks over against the speaker." Poetry, here, is no more "spontaneous overflow of powerful emotions."

If the dramatic monologues presented unique, if not verging on the neurotic, individual characters, much of Victorian poetry was preoccupied with individuals and their emotions. These poets demanded greater attention to the uniqueness of human character. The focus of interest was on the private self which was evacuated from the centre of culture by various social and ideological factors.

The Victorian poets also dealt with a startling variety of themes such as homicide, eroticism and irrelgion. Joseph Bristow points out that some of them "explored the darkest areas of the psyche, pushing on the limits of what was regarded as respectable" (*The Victorian Poet : Poetics and Persona*). For example, "Tennyson's hero in *Maud* (1855) fuses together sexual love with military ambition in tones that render violence and tenderness as almost wholly interchangeable" (*ibid.*), D.G. Rossetti's 'Jenny' (1870) describes a night spent by a man in the chamber of a prostitute after which he leaves her reflecting about both gaiety and shame, beauty and lust.

The Victorian poetry also dealt with the brutality of the mob, the minute details of the natural world and migration of labour. Whatever the theme, the poetry tended to be written in a diction "elevated above the level of ordinary speech, rich in sensuous imagery, well marked in rhythm and full in rhyme" (Messenger and Watson).

In spite of the rapidly growing phenomenon of urbanisation, the city remains conspicuously absent from much of the Victorian poetry. This neglect of the city and its hustle and bustle may be an inheritance from the Romantic movement. It may also have been a result of the prevalent conceptions of the poet and his art as well as of the importance of the traditional poetic language. At any rate, "the prevailing tone of much Victorian poetry is lassitude and weariness" (Messenger and Watson).

Major Poets of the Period

Alfred Lord Tennyson (1809-92)

Tennyson may be regarded as the representative poet of the period as we find him grappling with the fundamental questions of faith, doubt and immortality in his poems. However, "his genius was lyrical," as Auden points out. Hence his poetry does not provide so much instruction as enjoyment and inspiration. But the artist's duty, after all, is to provide enjoyment and inspiration.

His theme, says W.J. Long, "is the reign of order — of law in the physical world, producing evolution, and of law in the spiritual world, working out the perfect man." The law implies the existence of a divine source. The supreme purpose of all law is to reveal divine love. Thus all earthly love becomes an image of the heavenly. "Because law and love are in the world, faith is the only reasonable attitude toward life and death, even though we understand them not" (Long). Tennyson's major theme may thus be stated briefly. But his lyrical power is what actually adds both persuasiveness and beauty to his poetry.

Robert Browning (1812-89)

Browning mainly dealt with the unique individual human soul. He delved into the deepest psyche of the individual and sought to express the hidden motives and principles which govern individual action. The best technique he used for achieving his goal was the dramatic monologue, although he wrote also pure dramas like *Strafford* and dramatic narratives like *Pippa Passes*.

Browning is said to be an optimist. His is not the naive optimism of Pippa, who says :

> God's in His heaven —
> All's right with the world!

True, he believes with Rabbi Ben Ezra that "The best is yet to be." He, like Tennyson, "finds in love the supreme purpose and meaning of life" (Long), and his optimism springs from that belief. It is this optimism which leads him to believe that the individual will can overcome all obstacles.

Browning's poems do not have the lyrical beauty of Tennyson's poems. They have a rugged rhythm and colloquial vigour, both of which add splendour to the dramatic force of the poems.

Matthew Arnold (1822-88)

Arnold was very sensitive to the conflicts which existed in the Victorian England : the conflict between faith and doubt, emotion and reason, tradition and innovation. His poems usually start with a partly symbolic scene and then "in setting forth his spiritual troubles he seeks first of all to achieve a true and adequate statement, bare of non-essential decoration" (Douglas Bush).

e.g., Yes! in the sea of life enisl'd,
With echoing straits between us thrown,
Dotting with shoreless watery wild,
We mortal millions live alone. ('To Marguerite')

Written usually in a characteristically plain language, the poems tend to have diction and rhythm which are not great enough, as Bush says :

Arnold believes that poetry, while being an art, must also be a criticism of life.

13

Tithonus

ALFRED TENNYSON (1809-92)

The woods decay, the woods decay and fall.
The vapours weep their burden to the ground,
Man comes and tills the field and lies beneath,
And after many a summer dies the swan.
Me only cruel immortality
Consumes : I wither slowly in thine arms,
Here at the quite limit of the world,
A white-hair'd shadow roaming like a dream
The ever-silent spaces of the East,
Far folded mists, and gleaming halls of morn.

Alas! for this grey shadow, once a man —
So glorious in his beauty and thy choice,
Who madest him thy chosen, that he seem'd
To his great heart none other than a God!
I ask'd thee, "Give me immortality."
Then didst thou grant mine asking with a smile,
Like wealthy men who care not how they give.
But thy strong Hours indignant work'd their wills,
And beat me down and marr'd and wasted me,
And tho' they could not end me, left me maim'd.

To dwell in presence of immortal youth,
Immortal age beside immortal youth,
And all I was in ashes. Can thy love
Thy beauty make amends, tho' even now,
Close over us, the silver star, thy guide,

Shines in those tremulous eyes that fill with tears
To hear me? Let me go : take back thy gift :
Why should a man desire in any way
To vary from the kindly race of men,
Or pass beyond the goal of ordinance.

Where all should pause, as is most meet for all?
A soft air fans the cloud apart; there comes
A glimpse of that dark world where I was born.
Once more the old mysterious glimmer steals
From thy pure brows, and from thy shoulders pure,
And bosom beating with a heart renew'd.
Thy cheek begins to redden thro' the gloom,
Thy sweet eyes brighten slowly close to mine,
Ere yet they blind the stars, and the wild team
Which love thee, yearning for thy yoke, arise.

And shake the darkness from their loosen'd manes,
And beat the twilight into flakes of fire.
Lo! ever thus thou growest beautiful
In silence, then before thine answer given
Departest, and thy tears are on my cheek.
Why wilt thou ever scare me with thy tears,
And make me tremble lest a spying learnt,
In days far-off, on that dark earth, be true?
"The Gods themselves cannot recall their gifts."

Ay me! ay me! with what another heart
In days far-off, and with what other eyes
I used to watch — if I be he that watch'd —
The lucid outline forming round thee; saw
The dim curls kindle into sunny rings;
Changed with thy mystic change, and felt my blood
Glow with the glow that slowly crimson'd all
Thy presence and thy portals, while I lay,
Mouth, forehead, eyelids, growing dewy-warm
With kisses balmier than half-opening buds
Of April, and could hear the lips that kiss'd

Whispering I knew not what of wild and sweet,
Like that strange song I heard Apollo sing,

While Ilion like a mist rose into towers.
Yet hold me not for ever in thine East :
How can my nature longer mix with thine?
Coldly thy rosy shadows bathe me, cold
Are all thy lights, and cold my wrinkled feet
Upon thy glimmering thresholds; when the steam
Floats up from those dim fields about the homes
Of happy men that have the power to die,

And grassy barrows of the happier dead.
Release me, and restore me to the ground;
Thou seest all things, thou wilt see my grave :
Thou wilt renew thy beauty morn by morn;
I earth in earth forget these empty courts,
And thee returning on thy silver wheels.

Critical Appreciation

A sense of loss pervades much of Tennyson's poetry. James Spedding in 1835 said of his friend Tennyson that he was "a man always discontented with the Present till it has become the Past, and then he yearns towards it and worships it, and not only worships it, but is discontented because it is past." A similar worship of and a discontentment with the past pervades the poem, 'Tithonus.' The poem is a dramatic monologue (see the essay on the next poem, 'My Last Duchess,' for an explanation of 'dramatic monologue') in which "cadence, phrase, and image combine to produce the characteristic Tennysonian sense of loss" (David Daiches). The poem is about an immortal but senile lover who regrets the loss of his youth which had enabled him to live in a heaven of erotic ease. Having lost his youth he can only lament his immortality. The theme of the poem is characteristically Tennysonian : loss and the subjective crisis provoked by the loss.

The scene of the poem, as Stoppard A Brooke points out, is "laid in a dim, unknown country, on the outskirts of the heaven and the earth, below the visible, where there (is) no landscape." Its world is not a world of night or day, but of the transitory dawn.

The opening line of the poem underscores the transitoriness of life on the earth : "The woods decay, the woods decay and fall." Death is the ultimate law of nature. Even the clouds have to shed their life to the ground in the form of rains. Man's life on the earth is brief; its culmination is death. Even the beautiful white swan has to succumb to the ultimate law of nature. Tithonus laments that he alone has been condemned, against the law of nature, to immortality. Aurora, the goddess of dawn, had granted him immortality for the asking, but without youth. Hence, he is now "withering" although he still lives with the eternally young goddess in, her abode of the eastern horizon. Tithonus sees himself as "A white-hair'd shadow roaming like a dream." He feels that he has become as unsubstantial as a shadow, if not as unreal as a dream. He belongs to the no-where land of the eastern horizon, an area which belongs neither to heaven not to the earth. He is neither divine nor human.

Tithonus looks back into the past and recollects, with regret over its loss, the time when he belonged to the world of man. He was a man "So glorious in his beauty" that Aurora made him her choice and thus raised him to the status of a god. In order to confirm his divine status he asked Aurora for the gift of immortality, which she granted happily and spontaneously, without thinking of the consequences of her generosity as wealthy men may give away certain things arbitrarily. The arbitrary generosity of Aurora had a grave drawback : her gift of immortality was unaccompanied with youth. Hence, time wreaked its usual havoc on Tithonus. He remained immortal, but "marr'd and wasted" by senility. "Maim'd" by the ravages of time, he was pathetically condemned to live along with the eternally young Aurora. Tennyson contrasts the conditions of Tithonus and Aurora in the brilliant line : "Immortal age beside immortal youth."

Despite his senility, Tithonus is still loved by Aurora. However, Tithonus is not certain whether that love can ever rectify his error of having decided to differ from the "race of men" by his acquisition of immortality. His present condition is so pathetic that the morning star, Venus, is moved to tears as she listens to him. He asks Aurora to take back her gift of immortality. He sadly realises that a man should never desire to surpass the law of nature.

As Robert Pattison explains, Tithonus' unworthiness is not simply that he asked for immortality, "but that he gave up his whole being to his love, which provoked him to make his request... Tithonus has succumbed to love so completely that he has laid aside his duty as a man." The human duty is submission of the self to the larger forces of nature and time. Tithonus in his love for Aurora repudiated that duty entirely. The consequence is his dreadful inability to love and the equally dreadful inability to die.

From his abode in the eastern horizon Tithonus looks at the "dark world," the earth, which is his birth place. The darkness of the earth, unlike that of his own senile life, is temporary. Soon the earth will be bright with the ever-new brilliance that will radiate from Aurora's "pure brows" and "shoulders pure." Although incapable of sensuous love, Tithonus nostalgically describes the sensuous beauty of Aurora, of dawn, who reveals herself as the veil of the glimmering twilight is withdrawn. The eastern horizon grows red and bright, and the brightness will soon blind the stars which are still visible faintly. The horses that draw the chariot of Aurora have woken up "yearning for (her) yoke." As they shake their manes and get ready for yet another but ever-new trip, the twilight is beaten out and the bright crimson light of dawn spreads across the sky. Aurora keeps growing more and more beautiful with her reddening cheeks and brightening eyes. But she does not answer Tithonus, request for the revoking of her gift. Instead, she departs on her chariot having planted a kiss on his cheek. The tears frighten Tithonus because they forebode the painful veracity of a saying he has heard on the earth : "The Gods themselves cannot recall their Gifts."

Left alone now, after the tearful departure of Aurora, Tithonus reminisces about the bygone days when he used to observe the emergence of Aurora with a totally different state of mind. He even wonders whether he was the same man then as he is now. Those were the days when the sight of Aurora would fill his heart with rapture. He would watch her shadowy figure gradually emerging from the horizon and becoming bright and well-defined. Her "mystic change" would transform the dim clouds into "sunny rings." Tithonus would feel the warmth of love in his blood, as the eastern sky would be suffused with the crimson rays of the dawn.

> Soon his mouth, forehead and eyelids would grow dewy-warm
>
> With kisses balmier than half-opening buds of April.

He could also hear the rapturous music whispered by those luscious lips, music as enchanting as that which was played by Apollo in order to charm stones into appropriate places while he, along with Neptune, erected the walls of Troy.

Tithonus was the son of Laomedon, King of Troy. Mythology has it, that Apollo and Neptune were condemned by Zeus to serve Laomedon for a year. During this period they built the walls of Troy (Ilion). It is said that the stones of the walls were charmed into their places by the music from Apollo's lute. Tennyson compares Aurora's music to Apollo's. The implication is that Aurora's music could potentially enchant stones, let alone Tithonus, a young man of flesh and blood.

The reminiscence of the past only sharpens Tithonus' present frustration. He begs Aurora not to keep him eternally with her in her abode. "How can my nature longer mix with thee?" he asks. He cannot feel the same old passion, the ecstasy, any more. When Aurora's warmth vapourises the moisture in the distant fields, Tithonus remains cold at her "glimmering thresholds" incapable of feelings. The condition of a man who is unable to accept the offer of passionate love is indeed pathetic. It is this condition that prompts Tithonus to make the desperate observation about "the happy men that have the power to die." He begs for release from immortality. He yearns to be restored to the earth. Immortality is fit for Aurora who will "renew (her) beauty morn by morn." But Tithonus, with his ageing body, belongs to the earth. He longs to die and be buried in the earth oblivious of the regenerating beauty of Aurora and her eternal journey.

The interchanging play of memory and desire is a recurrent poetic strategy of Tennyson, says A.J. Carr. Desire and anxiety of youth become memory and regret of old age. The desirable future and the frustrations of the present come forth as the vanished past — recapturable in memory. The thirst of youth is presented as the dryness of age. The feelings of guilt inseparable from dream are costumed as remorse and self-reproach for what is gone and cannot be helped.

"Tennyson's poetry offers an analysis of the symptoms of the frustration rather than the cure," Carr goes on to argue. The frustration of Tithonus, like that of many Tennysonian characters, cannot be overcome unless Tithonus frees himself from fantasy and despair. This freedom, Tithonus is not able to achieve. That is why, he fails to be a tragic character despite his tragic situation.

14

My Last Duchess

ROBERT BROWNING (1812-89)

Ferrara

That's my last Duchess painted on the wall,
Looking as if she were alive; I call
That piece a wonder, now : Fra Pandolf's hands
Worked busily a day, and there she stands.
Will't please you sit and look at her? I said
"Fra Pandolf" by design, for never read
Strangers like you that pictured countenance,
The depth and passion of its earnest glance,
But to myself they turned (Since none puts by
The curtain I have drawn for you, but I)
And seemed as they would ask me, if they durst,
How such a glance came there; so, not the first
Are you to turn and ask thus. Sir, 'twas not
Her husband's presence only, called that spot
Of joy into the Duchess' cheek : perhaps
Fra Pandolf chanced to say "Her mantle laps
"Over my Lady's wrist too much," or "Paint
"Must never hope to reproduce the faint
"Half-flush that dies along her throat;" such stuff
was courtesy, she thought, and cause enough
For calling up that spot of joy. She had
A heart...how shall I say? ... too soon made glad,
Too easily impressed; she liked whate'er
She looked on, and her looks went everywhere.

Sir, 'twas all one! My favour at her breast,
The dropping of the daylight in the West,
The bough of cherries some officious fool
Broke in the orchard for her, the white mule
She rode with round the terrace — all and each
Would draw from her alike the approving speech,
Or blush, at least. She thanked men, — good; but thanked
Somehow.... I know not how...as if she ranked
My gift of a nine-hundred-years-old name
With anybody's gift. Who'd stoop to blame
This sort of trifling? Even had you skill
In speech — (which I have not) — to make your will
Quite clear to such an one, and say "Just this
"Or that in you disgusts me; here you miss,
"Or there exceed the mark" — and if she let
Herself be lessoned so, nor plainly set
Her wits to yours, forsooth, and made excuse,
- E'en then would be some stooping, and I choose
Never to stoop. Oh, Sir, she smiled, no doubt,
Whene'er I passed her; but who passed without
Much the same smile? This grew; I gave commands
Then all smiles stopped together. There she stands
As if alive. Will't please you rise? We'll meet
The company below, then. I repeat,
The Count your Master's known munificence
Is ample warrant that no just pretence
Of mine for dowry will be disallowed;
Though his fair daughter's self, as I avowed
At starting, is my object. Nay, we'll go
Together down, Sir : Notice Neptune, though,
Taming a sea-horse, thought a rarity,
Which Claus of Innsbruck cast in bronze for me.

Critical Appreciation

Robert Browning is well-known for his dramatic monologues. M.H. Abrams lists the following as the characteristics of a dramatic monologue :

1. A single person, who is not the poet himself, utters the entire poem in a specific situation at a critical moment.

2. This person addresses and interacts with one or more other people; but we know of the auditors' presence and what they say and do only from clues in the discourse of the single speaker.

3. The monologue is so organized that its focus is on the temperament and character that the dramatic speaker unintentionally reveals in the course of what he says.

(*A Glossary of Literary Terms*)

'My Last Duchess' is a dramatic monologue and the speaker is the Duke of Ferrara. In all probability the Duke was suggested by Alfonso II, fifth Duke of Ferrara, who married a girl of fourteen and then left her for two years. She then returned to the Duke, and after a year or so she died under mysterious circumstances.

Ferrara is an Italian city which was well-known for its culture and civilisation during the Renaissance. The Duke's character, in the poem, is marked by an aesthetic sense that has been nurtured by a sophisticated culture. But the Duke also reveals other aspects of his character such as his arrogance, possessiveness of his wife, and lack of human feelings. In the words of J M Cohen, this poem is "a study in that vitality and unscrupulousness, that luxury and love of art, that cruelty and subtlety, he (Browning) always associated with Italy and Renaissance" (*Robert Browning*).

Like most of Browning's dramatic monologues, 'My Last Duchess' opens at a critical juncture of the speaker's life, although the critical situation is made explicit only towards the end of the poem, and that serves to heighten the dramatic element in the monologue. The Duke is speaking to the envoy of a Count whose daughter he intends to marry. He shows a picture of his last Duchess to the envoy and speaks about her. It is not by accident that he speaks about his dead wife; he wants to impress upon the envoy and his master, the Count, about the kind of behaviour expected from his wife as well as about his own greatness.

The poem opens dramatically with the line, “That’s my last Duchess, painted on the wall.” The Duke’s speech then provides brilliant insights into his character and into the intricate psychological motivations of human nature. We also get a fairly clear idea about the Duchess’ character. Ironically, the picture we form of the Duchess is quite opposite to the one that the Duke portrays. This is true of the Duke’s portrait of himself too; he is not what he apparently presents himself to be.

The Duke, first, speaks about the quality of the painting in which the Duchess looks “as if she were alive.” He proudly declares that it has been painted by an eminent artist, Fra Pandolf. The painting, which is a piece of wonder, was accomplished in just one day. The envoy, is made to sit and admire it. The Duke observes the reaction of the envoy upon seeing the expression of the Duchess in the painting, and says that everyone who saw the painting had looked at him with a suppressed question in their eyes. The question obviously was how such a deep and passionate expression happened to be there, in the earnest eyes of the Duchess.

The Duke arrogantly explains that such an expression was generated on the Duchess’ face not just by the presence of her husband. He makes it appear that the Duchess would have blushed at the minutest attention paid to her by anybody. According to him, the expression would have been produced if the painter happened to remark that her cloak was covering too great a part of her wrist implying that her beauty was being concealed too much by the cloak. Or, the painter might have said that he could never succeed in reproducing the soft rosy tint suffusing the throat of the Duchess and fading away along her neck. Such trivial compliments, says the Duke, were taken seriously as signs of appreciation and esteem by the Duchess, and were sufficient to bring a blush of happiness to her cheeks. “She had/A heart,” says the Duke, “too soon made glad/Too easily impressed.” In short, she lacked the dignity that befitted a duchess.

Whatever the Duke may say, the picture of the Duchess that emerges from the monologue is one of an innocent young girl who enjoyed a spontaneous and compassionate oneness with other creatures. "Her naive acceptance of the obvious flattery of Fra Pandolf, who calls the blush to her cheeks as much for perverse sexual pleasure as for art, is hardly to be construed as a revelation of the poverty of her intellect," says Norton B Crowell in *The Triple Soul* : *Browning's Theory of Knowledge.* Perhaps, the Duchess never blushed at all, as Crowell surmises, because she must have been "aware of the imperious decree of her husband that the painter finish the portrait in a single day as a means of occupying hands suspected of dexterity in the art of love as well as of painting." In that case, the blush is the painter's addition to her face. The point that the Duke wishes to make, however, is that his wife had a heart which was "too soon made glad," "too easily impressed." The Duke being a man of heartless calculation can only "despise the signs of common humanity in others" (Crowell).

The Duke's hesitated expression — "how shall I say?" — is intended to create a favourable impression of him on the listener. Instead of stating bluntly that the Duchess was a fickle-hearted woman with no sense of judgement or restraint — which is what the Duke wants the listener to gather, he hesitates and then expresses his thoughts in as delicate a phraseology as possible. The listener, if he is intelligent enough, will realise that the Duke is wearing a mask, that he is hiding his real self, "a self made insanely jealous by a wife who 'liked whate'er/She looked on' and whose 'looks went everywhere'" (Betty S. Flowers).

The Duke is constantly trying to build up a desirable image of himself, as Flowers argues in *Browning and the Modern Tradition.* His strategy is to utter an apparent praise about something in the Duchess' character, then attack that quality which has been praised and substantiate the attack with sufficient reasons intended to convince the listener about the Duchess' deficiency as well as the Duke's greatness. But the Duke will fail in his attempt at self-glorification or even self-justification, because his basic nature of callousness; arrogance and crude jealousy is transparent in spite of the mask he puts on. His excessive concern with aristocratic decorum and dignity leaves even the masked face without any trace of humanity.

One of the major deficiencies of the Duchess, according to the Duke, is her absolute lack of sense of discrimination. Although we can see her as a simple soul who has an "approving speech" for "all and each," the Duke wants us to think of her as a woman without refined tastes of propriety. She could be pleased as easily by the sight of a routine sunset as by a special gift of the Duke. "Some officious fool" who offered her a gift of cherries, or the mule on which she rode around would receive from her the same kind of appreciation as she would proffer to the Duke for his precious gifts. She thanked men profusely. Her sense of gratitude did not seem to discriminate between the rank and file and the Duke whose ancestral history went back to nine centuries.

The Duke refused to tell his wife about her indecorous behaviour as he regarded it beneath his dignity to have to speak to his wife about such obvious matters. Even if he had the eloquence to convince her, and even if she was very amenable to such exhortations, he would not try doing anything of the sort as it "would be some stooping" and he has chosen "never to stoop."

The Duke could not tolerate his wife's generosity with her smile too. She did smile at him, and the smiles were sweet indeed. "....but who passed without/Much the same smile?" asks the Duke superciliously. Finally a time came when the Duke could not put up with what he saw as a lack of decorum and discretion, and gave the order : "Then all smiles stopped together."

Having given his version of the Duchess' character, the Duke asks the envoy to accompany him downstairs where the other members of the Count's party are waiting. On the way he does not hesitate to suggest that he expects a large dowry from the Count. Before leaving the room, he also calls the attention of the envoy to a rare bronze statue of Neptune taming a sea-horse and proudly remarks that the statue was specially made for him by Claus of Innsbruck.

It is only towards the end of the poem that we come to know of the actual purpose of the envoy's visit. The revelation now, that he has come with a marriage proposal for the Duke, comes as a denouement of the drama in the poem. "Like the born story-teller that he is," says Ian Jack, "Browning keeps a surprise for the end : a surprise that is not a mere structural device, since it throws a retrospective light on the monologue as a whole."

Browning's dramatic monologues, in the works of David Daiches, "project...a certain kind of personality, a certain temperament, a way of looking at life, even a moment of history realized in the self-revelation of a type." 'My Last Duchess' presents an arrogant Duke of the Renaissance Italy. The Duke is proud to the extent of being vain about his family name, his position and his aesthetic sense. The thinks that he bestowed a supreme favour on the Duchess by marrying her and giving her his centuries — old family name.

It is his vanity that makes him intolerant of the simple good nature of the Duchess. As W.L. Phelps says, the Duchess must have been "a frank, charming girl, who came from a happy home, a bright and eager bride, who was one of those lovely women whose kindness and responsiveness are as natural as the sunlight." She was unpretentious woman who took delight in watching a sunset, or petting her white mule. The Duke is incapable of perceiving such simple goodness, let alone appreciating it, because he is spiritually dead. He cannot see people as people. "His pride in station and possession," says R.E. Gridley, "has led him to treat people as possessions, objects, things. The Last Duchess has become a mere art-object and the envoy a tool to be used." The envoy is the person through whom the Duke intimates his new bride and his expectations of his wife.

The Duke was extremely, even jealously, possessive of his wife. He considered her to be his personal property, like any of his art piece. He denied her the right of individuality. When she would behave as the distinct individual that she was, the Duke would find her intolerable. She finally became a tragic victim of his tyranny. The Duke's heartlessness, his spiritual death, is obvious from his callous comment on the painting : "There she stands/As if alive." He prefers the life seen in art to that in reality.

The Duke's tyrannical nature is reasserted in his inviting the envoy's attention to the bronze statue. The statue of Neptune taming a sea-horse "acts as a reminder that the Duke intends to 'tame' the new Duchess" (Gridley).

In his book, *Browning's Major Poetry*, Ian Jack raises a question whether the Duke is insane. Browning was particularly interested in insanity and every sort of mental imbalance, says Jack. But when a character portrayed is insane, Browning somehow draws our attention to that fact. The Duke is not insane; he is a man who is "almost frighteningly in charge of the situation."

The metre and the rhyme of the poem also help to highlight the menacing character of the Duke. Browning has used "boldly enjambed pentameter couplets, with the rhyme so muted that it affects us at a subconscious rather than a conscious level. " Jack rightly asserts that "this helps to...enhance our feeling that the Duke is as sane a man as Iago."

15

Dover Beach

MATTHEW ARNOLD (1822-88)

The sea is clam tonight.
The tide is full, the moon lies fair
Upon the straits; — on the French coast the light
Gleams and is gone; the cliffs of England stand,
Glimmering and vast, out in the tranquil bay.
Come to the window, sweet is the night-air!
Only, from the long line of spray
Where the sea meets the moon-blanch'd land,
Listen! You hear the grating roar
Of pebbles which the waves draw back, and fling,
At their return, up the high strand,
Begin, and cease, and then again begin,
With tremulous cadence slow, and bring
The eternal note of sadness in.

Sophocles long ago
Heard it on the Aegean, and it brought
Into his mind the turbid ebb and flow
Of human misery; we
Find also in the sound a thought,
Hearing it by this distant northern sea.

The sea of faith
Was once, too, at the full, and round earth's shore
Lay like the folds of a bright girdle furl'd.
But now I only hear
Its melancholy, ling, withdrawing roar,

Retreating, to the breath
Of the night-wind, down the vast edges drear
And naked shingles of the world.

Ah, love, let us be true
To one another! For the world, which seems
To lie before us like a land of dreams,
So various, so beautiful, so new,
Hath really neither joy, nor love, nor light,
Nor certitude, nor peace, nor help for pain;
And we are here as on a darkling plain
Swept with confused alarms of struggle and flight,
Where ignorant armies clash by night.

Critical appreciation

'Dover Beach' is a typical Arnoldian poem because opening with a natural scene which has a symbolic function, the poem goes on to express the melancholy of a man who oscillates between time and eternity, doubt and faith. Moreover, the diction of the poem is essentially Arnoldian : a mixture of the poetic and the prosaic.

The setting of the poem, vividly outlined in the stanza I, is a landscape in which the sea meets the land. However, the meeting is not one which enriches each of the entities that meet. The sea and the land remain separate in spite of the former's relentless attempt to make a lasting relationship with the latter. The outcome of each such attempt is a "grating roar."

The sea and the land as well as their meeting are symbolic. The sea is calm although the tide is full. It is the source of "sweet...night air." The music of its waves has a slow, regular rhythm that is soothing to human souls. The bay which is part of the sea is tranquil. The sea, in short, is the source of happiness and tranquility.

The land, on the other hand, gives a sense of uncertainty with the flickering light on the French coast and the glimmering cliffs on the English coast. There is a perceptible inconstancy in the appearance of the land. The land is a symbol of the Victorian ethos which was marked by many oscillations, much uncertainty.

The sea assumes a deeper meaning in the third stanza where the poet makes an equation between sea and faith. However, in the first stanza, the problem of lack of faith is only hinted at in the description of the land. There are no direct statements here regarding the problems the poet deals with in stanza three. The word "Listen!" does serve to awaken us from mere observation of sea and land to the harshness of the otherwise soothing music of the sea. The harshness is audible only to a discerning ear, to particularly attentive ear. It is produced when the waves draw pebbles from the shore and fling them back "up the high strand" as if the sea cannot ingest anything from the land. Much as the sea may long for a meaningful union with the land, it seems fated to remain separate because the two denote two different value systems. Hence, "the eternal note of sadness" in the music of the sea. The vast mystery represented by the sea is incompatible with the mundaneness of the land. "The eternal note of sadness," in the words of Murray Krieger, "is caused by the endless battle without victory and without truce between sea and land."

It is an endless battle. Sophocles heard the sad music of the battling ocean "long ago." The Sophocles of Arnold, as pointed out by Warren Anderson, is a composite figure. His moral greatness and artistic genius, "the even-balanced soul," represent the ideals which Arnold held up before himself. Human incarnations of such ideals are rare, though. That is the misery of human life. Arnold is awakened to thoughts about that "human misery" by the sad music of the sea.

The mention of Sophocles also serves to connect the past with the present, even as the word "eternal" serves to transcend the divisions of time into past, present and future. The first three lines of the third stanza take us back to a time when the land was surrounded by the secure "girdle" of "the sea of faith." Faith was then, a binding force; it helped each man to remain and integrated person, a person in whom there was no schism between faith and doubt, between emotion and reason, between spontaneity and discipline.

Gone are those days. This is Arnold's lament in the second

part of the stanza. The sea of faith is no more a binding girdle. Now the poet can

only hear
Its melancholy, ling, withdrawing roar.

It is withdrawing leaving only "naked shingles" on the land. The nakedness is nothing but the spiritual emptiness of man.

The last stanza is marked by a change in rhyme and rhythm. A definite rhyme scheme (abbacddcc) and lines of even length take the place of the irregular lines and rhymes of the first three stanzas. However, the problem presented in the poem is not resolved in the last stanza either, although there is a vague suggestion of a solution. The clash described earlier is endless indeed. The world is only apparently beautiful. It lies "before us like a land of dreams." In reality there is

neither joy, nor love, nor light,
Nor certitude, nor peace, nor help for pain.
The human beings are fated to live in a twilight zone
Swept with confused alarm of struggle and flight,
Where ignorant armies clash by night.

J.D. Jump regards the last line of the poem as "Arnold's most impressive and most pregnant poetic utterance on 'modern life.' There is a constant clash in the human soul. It makes the soul restless. It takes away joy, love, peace, and so on. Nevertheless, the cause of the clash is not very clear. It is like the fighting in the dark by ignorant armies. It is a purposeless fight. In the absence of faith, of spiritual moorings, the strain of the fight is indeed unbearable. The only solution to the problem seems to be loving fidelity.

Ah, love, let us be true
To one another!

The poem, 'Dover Beach,' was probably occasioned by Arnold's brief stay with his wife at Dover during their honeymoon in 1851. Hence, the invocation, 'love,' may be directed towards his wife. However, restraining from too personal a reading of the poem, we may agree with William A Madden that the love referred to is "the love of those who have shed romantic illusions in favour of a more realistic, more resigned companionship of mutually pledged fidelity in an infected world."

On the whole the poem remains an eloquent and moving expression of the condition of men who are facing a spiritual crisis. The images employed in the poem, both visual and auditory, as well as their interplay underscore the theme of endless conflict in the human soul. They also serve to increase our awareness of the problem gradually. We slowly become conscious of the exact nature of the endless tidal ebb and flow, of "the repetitive inclusiveness of the human condition and its purposeless gyrations" (Krieger). Thus, the form of the poem is in perfect harmony with its theme.

16

Twentieth Century Poetry : Introduction

Gerard Manley Hopkins lived in the nineteenth century. But as he can be said to be the usherer of modernism into English poetry, he is included among the twentieth century poets in this volume. His poetry marks a radical change from the Victorian poetry, especially in style, diction and technique. True, Hopkins did not make a complete break with the past. But he brought new rhythm and imagery into poetry. The thoughts and feelings in his poems also differ significantly from those in the earlier poetry.

Modernism can be said to have arisen from two movements : symbolism and imagism. Symbolism is a movement that originated in France in the nineteenth century (1880-95, approximately). Reacting against the realist and naturalist tendencies which were in vogue earlier, symbolism stressed the priority of suggestion and evocation over direct description and explicit analogy. They sought to achieve this through use of symbols and metaphors. The symbolists were particularly concerned to explore the musical properties of language. They did not care much for conventional metres and logical narratives.

Imagism (1910-17, approximately) revolted against Romanticism. It derived in part from the aesthetic philosophy of T.E. Hulme. Its characteristics may be summarized as follows :

1. Use of the language of common speech in poetry. However, it demanded the use of the exact word.
2. Creation of new rhythms which can express new moods.

3. Absolute freedom for the poet in choice of his subject matter.
4. Presentation of the matter through images. The images were meant to render particulars exactly instead of dealing with vague generalities.
5. Hard and clear poetry.
6. Concentration.

In short, imagism demanded poetry that renders visual experiences clearly and precisely.

Inspired by Symbolism and Imagism, the moderns demanded economy and concentration in style and diction. They also repudiated tidy logical exposition in poetry. In stead, they put ideas side by side, one after the other, without caring to arrange them in precise logical order. Life does not have any logical order, after all, as they realized. They also made generous use of metaphors, symbols and images. The relation between music and poetry was explored too.

Technically, modern poetry encouraged experimentalism. It rejected the traditional framework of narrative, description and rational exposition. The stream-of-consciousness presentation of personality is a favorite technique of the Moderns. Apart from images and symbols, myths became a frequently used tool. Primitive myths were made use of in grasping and ordering the chaos of modern life.

The Modern poets looked to the city for subject matter, although there was no restriction about choice of subject. However, the problems of the city dweller became an important consideration of these poets. Moreover, it was not the city in general, but the intelligentsia in the city that captured their attention.

The Modern poets believed that that the unconscious life was as important as the conscious life. Their interest in psychology was immense. They also believed that personality was precarious and fragmentary rather than substantial and unchanging. Hence, contradictions in experience were unavoidable, and poetry could accommodate these by ironic juxtaposition or superimposition.

Owing to the same reason, the Modern also believed that any final or absolute interpretation of literary works was impossible.

The Movement

'The Movement' is a term coined by J.D. Scott to describe a group of nine poets including Philip Larkin (whose one poem is included in this volume). The characteristics of their poetry may be summarized as follows :

1. Emphasis on clarity, intellectual detachment and formal perfection.
2. Belief in the "principle that poetry is written by and for the whole man, intellect, emotions, senses and all" (Robert Conquest).
3. Emphasis on the dignity of ordinary things.
4. Wry honesty and technical coolness.
5. Unemotional in approach to reality.
6. Avoidance of symbolism, abstractions and allegory.

17

Pied Beauty

GERARD MANLEY HOPKINS (1844-89)

Glory be to God for dappled things —
  For skies of couple-colour as a brinded cow;
    For rose-moles all in stipple upon trout that swim;
Fresh-firecoal chestnut-falls; finches' wings;
  Landscape plotted and pieced-fold, fallow, and plough;
    And all trades, their gear and tackle and trim.

All things counter, original, spare, strange;
  Whatever is fickle, freckled (who knows how?)
    With swift, slow; sweet, sour; adazzle, dim;
He fathers-forth whose beauty is past change :
                                        Praise him.

Critical Appreciation

Hopkins was extremely sensitive to the variegated beauty in nature and viewed objects of beauty as glorious manifestations of God, their creator. He possessed a peculiar sensibility which enabled him to have a penetrating vision, an ability to perceive the distinctive individuality of each thing as well as the relation that exists among different things. Hence, we can say that his vision was both microscopic and macroscopic.

The vision begins with individual objects which are apparently dissimilar, unrelated. But the relation that does exist among them becomes gradually obvious. The "single sovereign principle" (J. Hillis Miller's phrase) that reveals this relation is 'rhyme.' For Hopkins, this relation which exists among dissimilar things is beauty. Poetry reveals this beauty.

Since poetry reveals the 'rhyme' that exists among various objects of nature, it is a kind of music of words. "Music makes patterns of sequences of tones. Poetry makes patterns of sequences of words," says Miller. The words in a poem do not speak about the external world any more than do the notes in music. The function of poetry is rather to reveal the individual patterns of objects as well as the 'rhyme' that connects these patterns. The individual pattern is what Hopkins calls 'inscape.' The inner energy that upholds the individual pattern is labeled 'instress' by Hopkins. All things have inscape and instress. All things have unique individuality and relation with other individuals. Or, in the words of Miller, "The universe, Even though no two things in it are exactly alike, is full of things which rhyme." Hopkins perceives both the individuality and the rhyme, both inscape and in stress, and presents them through his poetry.

'Pied Beauty' is a poem which presents the "relation between things which are similar without being identical" (Miller). The various objects catalogued in the poem are related to one another by virtue of their being pied. The quality of piedness is not restricted to colour, though the objects listed in the first four lines seem to imply that. The mention of "fold, fallow, and plough," of trades and their gear in the succeeding lines as well as the adjectives "swift, slow," etc., towards the end indicate the wider significance of piedness.

The broad implication of piedness is articulated right at the beginning of the poem by the word "dappled." For Hopkins the word means much more than its literal meaning. Dapple is a quality which, as Peter Milward points out, "diversifies (objects) in almost unlimited individuality." Everything in nature is dappled, it seems, for Hopkins. He has applied that adjective to phenomena varying from dawn to apple blossoms. In 'Pied Beauty' there is a fairly long list of items which are dappled. What Hopkins tells us is that all beauty in the universe is "essentially 'pied beauty' — beauty that is intricately interwoven with white and black, light and darkness, summer and winter, day and night, heaven and earth" (Milward).

The particular dappled things mentioned by the poet are the sky with its dapple of blue and white, the cow with its shades of brown and white, the trout with its spotted configurations, broken chestnuts within which the seeds look like burning coal, and the multi-coloured wings of finches. The whole landscape looks pied as it consists of areas used for different purposes. One such area is the ploughed or, implicitly (because 'fallow' also means ploughed), the cultivated land, and its mention leads the poet to the works of man, his "trades," and to the mention of certain tools which are also dappled. Milward's interpretation of "gear and tackle and trim" is :

> ...the poet is evidently thinking of his preferred pastime of fishing, both on the individual scale of an angler, who needs 'tackle,' and on the wider scale of fishing-boats and trawlers, whose 'gear' has to be kept in good 'trim.'

If everything in the universe is dappled, why does the poet choose the items mentioned? Why not mention some things also which are, say, multi-coloured instead of 'couple-coloured'? For one thing, the poet has to choose a few objects which will symbolize the pied beauty of the universe, and Hopkins has chosen objects which 'rhyme' (in the sense of 'being related') as they all share some shade of red or brown. The more important reason is Hopkins' theory of poetry. If poetry is music of words, as seen earlier, the poet has to choose words which produce not just meaning but music. Thus, for example, 'cow' finds its place along with 'skies' because of the alliteration in the words 'skies,' 'couple-colour' and 'cow.' Similar alliterations exist in most lines of the poem. Thus, the 'rhyme' that exists among the objects is given life to by the poet through the music in his poem.

It may also be noted that the objects mentioned cover the four universal elements : earth, water, air and fire.

The poet apparently moves from the particular to the general in the second stanza. "All things" are called into the catalogue whether they are "counter, original, spare, strange." That is, "all things that stand in contrast with other things, that are unique in themselves, that are rarely to be found in the world, that arouse surprise when they are found or looked at afresh" (Milward). In spite of the similarity between things, the inscape of each thing makes it unique. The latter section of the poem is full of adjectives all of which suggest "subjective and objective qualities at the same time" (Miller). The perception of such qualities as swiftness, sweetness or dimness will vary from person to person, and hence they are subjective. But they are also objective as these qualities do belong to the objects perceived. If the objective clubs objects together under definite general categories such as the swift, the sweet, the dim, and so on, the subjectivity differentiates between any two items in the general category. Hence, we can say that Hopkins transcends particularization and generalization in this part of the poem, and thus moves from the microscopic to the macroscopic vision.

It is only natural that the macroscopic vision leads Hopkins to the underlying essential reality which is beyond classification, beyond measurable qualities, beyond change. That reality is God whose beauty it is that becomes manifest in the created objects. Hence, the call to praise God.

The first line of the poem also said much the same thing : "Glory be to God for dappled things." For Hopkins, a religious poet, God is the beginning and end of everything. The exhortation at the end of the poem has an additional meaning, however. It is best explained in the words of Miller :

> The poem works from the first line back around to an apparent repetition of it through an exploration of the nature of pied beauty in the middle lines. The last line is really repetition with a difference — it rhymes in meaning with the first line. At the end of the poem the reader knows that he did not simply say "Glory be to God for dappled things," blandly and naturally. By understanding the dappled or pied nature of the universe he best understands the nature of God, though God's beauty is past change, and this knowledge makes it possible to praise God. The whole poem leads up to the two words, which make up the final half line.

'Pied Beauty' is a devotional poem. In form it is what Hopkins calls a 'curtal sonnet.' A curtal sonnet is three-fourth the length of an ordinary sonnet, and consists of ten-and-a-half lines. It has its own 'octave' and 'sestet,' consisting respectively of six and four-and-a-half lines. In the octave of 'Pied Beauty'

Hopkins speaks of particular things, and in the sestet he moves through general qualities towards the ultimate reality, the source of the particular and the general, of the similar and the dissimilar.

In the final analysis, the poem is an exquisite song of praise to God as much for the multiplicity of His creation as for the relation that exists among the multiple objects. The various types of rhyme in the poem make the poem itself a 'pied beauty' besides reiterating the rhyme in the universe.

18

A Prayer for My Daughter

WILLIAM BUTLER YEATS (1865-1939)

Once more the storm is howling, and half hid
Under this cradle-hood and coverlid
My child sleeps on. There is no obstacle
But Gregory's wood and one bare hill
Whereby the haystack — and roof-levelling wind,
Bred on the Atlantic, can be stayed;
And for an hour I have walked and prayed
Because of the great gloom that is in my mind.

I have walked and prayed for this young child an hour
And heard the sea-wind scream upon the tower,
And under the arches of the bridge, and scream
In the elms above the flooded stream;
Imagining in excited reverie
That the future years had come,
Dancing to a frenzied drum
Out of the murderous innocence of the sea.

May she be granted beauty and yet not
Beauty to make a stranger's eye distraught,
Or hers before a looking-glass, for such,
Being made beautiful overmuch,
Consider beauty a sufficient end,
Lose natural kindness and maybe
The heart-revealing intimacy
That chooses right, and never find a friend.

Helen being chosen found life flat and dull
And later had much trouble from a fool,
While that great Queen, that rose out of the spray,
Being fatherless could have her way
Yet chose a bandy-legged smith for man.
It's certain that fine women eat
A crazy salad with their meat
Whereby the Horn of Plenty is undone.

In courtesy I'd have her chiefly learned;
Hearts are not had as a gift but hearts are earned
By those that are not entirely beautiful;
Yet many, that have played the fool
For beauty's very self, has charm made wise,
And many a poor man that has roved,
Loved and thought himself beloved,
From a glad kindness cannot take his eyes.

May she become a flourishing hidden tree
That all her thoughts may like the linnet be,
And have not business but dispensing round
Their magnanimities of sound,
Nor but in merriment begin to chase
Nor but in merriment a quarrel.
O may she live like some green laurel
Rooted in one dear perpetual place.

My mind, because the minds that I have loved,
The sort of beauty that I have approved,
Prosper but little, has dried up of late,
Yet knows that to be choked with hate
May well be of all evil chances chief.
If there's no hatred in a mind
Assault and battery of the wind
Can never tear the linnet from the leaf.

An intellectual hatred is the worst,
So let her think opinions are accursed.
Have I not seen the loveliest woman born
Out of the mouth of Plenty's horn,
Because of her opinionated mind

Barter that horn and every good
By quiet natures understood
For an old bellows full of angry wind?

Considering that, all hatred driven hence,
The soul recovers radical innocence
And learns at last that it is self-delighting,
Self-appeasing, self-affrighting,
And that its own sweet will is Heaven's will;
She can, though every face should scowl
And every windy quarter howl
Or every bellows burst; be happy still.

And may her bridegroom bring her to a house
Where all's accustomed, ceremonious;
For arrogance and hatred are the wares
Peddled in thoroughfares.
How but in custom and in ceremony
Are innocence and beauty born?
Ceremony's a name for the rich horn,
And custom for the spreading laurel tree.

Critical Appreciation

'A Prayer for My Daughter's is one of the poems in *Michael Robartes and the Dancer*, published in 1921. The poem apparently is a prayer for the poet's daughter, Anne Butler Yeats, born on Feb. 26, 1919. It opens with a mention of the chaos of the modern world and goes on to present Yeats' theories about women. In spite of the title, the theme of the poem is the real beauty of women as contrasted with physical beauty and intellectual abilities.

In the scene set in the opening stanza a storm is raging outside as the poet's child is sleeping in her cradle. There is nothing that can effectively resist the storm except "Gregory's wood[1] and one bare hill". The storm that originated in the Atlantic ocean may wreak a lot of havoc. The poet has been troubled in his mind for about an hour and he has been praying all that time.

The storm has a symbolic function and value. Yeats believed that history moved in vast two thousand year cycles, each cycle representing a civilization and each one ushered in by a dramatic religio-mystical revelation of some kind. For example, the Christian era (0-2000 A.D.) began with the annunciation of Mary and the birth of Christ as, earlier, the Graeco-Roman era (2000-0 B.C.) had begun with the annunciation of Leda and the birth of Helen. Yeats was sure that the twentieth century, of which he had seen the calamitous, beginning — World War I on the continent, and political troubles at home — would make the end of the Christian civilization. The storm described in the first stanza is a symbol of the chaos that will eventually bring about the end of the present civilization.

In the second stanza the storm imagery is extended from the physical world to the world of history. As the poet paces restlessly in his room praying for his infant daughter, he can hear the storm lashing against the tower[2]. The stream near his house is flooded and the storm can be heard screaming in the elms above the stream. The poet imagines.

> That the future years had come,
> Dancing to a frenzied drum,
> Out of the murderous innocence of the sea.

These lines with their ominous overtones as well as the symbolic storm are reminiscent of Yeats's another poem, 'The Second Coming', which appears just before 'A Prayer for My Daughter, in the volume. 'The Second Coming' is about the violent end of our civilization as foreseen by the poet.

> Things fall apart; the center cannot hold;
>
> Mere anarchy is loosed upon the world,
> The blood-dimmed tide is loosed, and everywhere
> The ceremony of innocence is drowned.

Innocence which is not a ceremony, a ritual, can be dangerous, "murderous." Yeats speaks about "radical innocence" in stanza 9. In the words of Harold Bloom, "Radical innocence...is the soul's solipsistic knowledge of its own autonomy, and is born only out of ritual." In other words, radical innocence is a virtue that belongs only to that soul which has been nurtured by the wisdom of the ages. The external behaviour of such a soul will be marked by such formal qualities as courtesy, etiquette and customary graces. Such refinement, however, is vanishing from our civilization in which "the ceremony of innocence" gets drowned.

The innocence of the sea is murderous because it is not accompanied with the wisdom of an enlightened soul. Having spoken of the innocent murderousness of the sea, Yeats moves on to the undesirable kind of beauty in women (stanzas 3 and 4). Both are born out of ignorance. Bloom's observation in this context is significant :

> As Yeats moves, with no transition, to the thought of Maud Gonne's beauty, and her archetype, Helen's, it is a reasonable surmise that one "innocence" in the poem is being redefined persuasively, to mean a quality closely associated with a woman's murderous beauty. But this innocence, of sea or of Maud Gonne, Helen and the sea-born Aphrodite, is what Blake called "unorganized," and therefore an "impossibility," because it dwells with ignorance and not with wisdom. The higher, organized innocence of Blake Yeats calls "radical," and presumably it cannot be murderous.

From stanza 3 onwards the poem elaborates Yeats's views about the virtues that a woman ought to possess. At first he speaks about a kind of beauty that can be 'murderous' and hence undesirable. Mere physical beauty, which some women regard as an end in itself, does more harm than good. Women who possess such beauty :

> Lose natural kindness and maybe
> The heart-revealing intimacy
> That chooses right, and never find a friend.

Women who are physically beautiful can enchant men. Men can be driven mad ("distraught") with the heart-ache of love. Yeats says that he would not wish his daughter to be physically so beautiful that, looking at herself in the mirror, she should forget the more important virtues such as natural kindness and emotional warmth, and come to regard physical beauty as an end in itself.

The poet mentions examples of women who were physically

very beautiful but lacked certain essential human qualities. Helen of Troy is one such woman who was very proud of her beauty. Pride made her life with her husband, Menelaus, dull. She ran away with Paris, a Trojan prince. Her elopement led to a prolonged war between the Greeks and Trojans. Aphrodite is another woman referred to by the poet. Goddess of beauty and love, she is believed to have emerged from the sea-foam. Having had no father, she knew no discipline and was led by her whims. She married the lame god, Hephaestus, and was unhappy in life. Subsequently she developed a love affair with another god. The poet concludes that such beautiful women have some crazy notion or the other which leads them ultimately to destruction, to the 'undoing' of the "Horn of Plenty."

The horn of plenty is the mythological cornucopia, and unexhausting source of flowers, fruits and corn. It denotes prosperity and plenty. It is one of the three major symbols employed in the poem. Yeats mentions it in stanzas 4, 8 and 10. In stanza 4, the horn is pitted against the arrogant physical beauty which regards itself as an end, and it serves as a symbol of such virtues as kindness and emotional warmth. Later, in stanza 8, it becomes a symbol of intellectual virtues when Yeats contrasts it with the intellectual hatred and opinionated mind of "the loveliest woman born." Finally, "the rich horn" is equated with "ceremony" (stanza 10). Thus, it is symbolically the source of all emotional, intellectual and traditional values, of the kind of beauty and grace with which a women ought to be blessed.

Having dismissed as undesirable physical beauty unaccompanied with certain emotional virtues, the poet now prays for another virtue that his daughter, like every good woman, ought to possess : courtesy. Mere physical beauty cannot win over hearts. "Hearts are not had as a gift but hearts are earned," says the poet.

The fifth stanza also contains references to two women, one an epitome of vain beauty, and the other of "glad kindness." The first reference is to Maud Gonne. Yeats devoted himself to wooing her for about twenty years. He is the

Poor man that has roved,
Loved and thought himself beloved.

Gonne was a beautiful actress who became a revolutionary nationalist. She apparently felt that Yeats was too idealistic to be the right husband for her. Yeats regarded her as a woman made proud by her beauty. The second reference is to Georgie Hydelees, Yeats's wife, who was very understanding towards her husband.

The poet then prays that his daughter must attain victory in life by being virtuous. He wants her to be like the laurel tree, which is a symbol of victory. The tree remains "Rooted in one dear perpetual place". It may be "hidden" but it is "flourishing." The poet also wishes that his daughter be like the song-bird, linnet, spreading joyful and magnanimous "sound." He would not have his daughter entering into arguments or quarrels with others except for "merriment." The poet's prayer now is that his daughter be victorious in life by spreading joy and happiness around. There is a fair hint that this will be possible only if she is rooted in an aristocratic tradition which is a major moulding force of a woman's real beauty.

The laurel tree is the second major symbol in the poem. The laurels are traditionally leaves of victory. F.A.C. Willson sees it as the tree of life itself. He substantiates his argument by referring to Daphne. In classical mythology Daphne, daughter of the river-god, Peneus, was metamorphosed into a laurel tree. In Yeatsean vision, all material reality is an expression of the ultimate reality. The laurel tree, the metamorphosed form of divinity, is a symbol of the Unity of Being.

In the next stanza the poet presents another virtue that the ideal woman ought to possess : intellectual innocence. In order to spread joy and happiness around, one's mind must be fee of hate, both emotional and intellectual hate. The mind that is free of hatred can easily withstand the destructive forces in the world. The chief evil, according to the poet, is "to be choked with hate." The poet mentions that his own mind "has dried up of late" because the people whom he loved, the women whose beauty he approved of, have not prospered much in life. The reference is again to Maud Gonne.

Continuing the reference to Maud Gonne, the poet says that he has seen "the loveliest woman born" destroying herself because of her "intellectual hatred" and opinionated mind. "An intellectual hatred is the worst," asserts the poet. Women who possess such hatred exchange their horn of plenty, the source of all good things, with "an old bellows full of angry wind." The bellows is a symbol of futile anger which is a curse in women. It is the opposite of the horn of plenty.

Shorn of hatred, one's soul becomes the seat of one's joy and peace. Such souls fulfill the will of God. They can withstand all evil forces and thus be always happy.

The last stanza reveals Yeats's tradition-oriented, aristocratic view of life. He wants his daughter to marry an aristocrat in whose house customs and ceremonies will be followed. In such houses there will be no place for "arrogance and hatred." Innocence and beauty are products of custom and ceremony. Custom is the established tradition which gives order, grace and peace to life. Ceremony is the whole complex of civilized courtesy which forms the foundation of aristocratic life.

"Throughout his life," says Louis MacNeice, "his (Yeats's) advice to women is to abjure the intellect and, in particular, political opinions and the critical reason. Their discipline is to be that of the looking-glass."

> bear in mind your lover's wage
> Is what your looking-glass can show,

says Michael Robartes to the dancer in Yeats's title poem of the volume in which 'A Prayer for My Daughter' occurs. Michael Robartes insists that women should rely on the spontaneous genius of their beauty rather than on learning. "A prayer for My Daughter" states clearly the kind of beauty Yeats expected in women. The poem delineates the ideal woman in Yeats's view.

Fitting in with the theme, the poem makes use of a rhyme scheme which Yeats perfected : aabbcddc. The same rhyme is used in "Major Gregory," Yeats's poem about the ideal man.

Each stanza consists of eight lines and the tone and diction are formal and dignified. The allusions to mythology and the use of classical symbols and images render a peculiar solemnity to the poem.

1. Lady Gregory was the widow of an Anglo-Irish land-owner. Yeats met her in 1896 at Coole, her estate. The two became good friends.
2. The poem is set in Ballylee, Yeats's castle (tower) near the Gregory estate.

19

The Love Song of J. Alfred Prufrock

THOMAS STEARNS ELIOT (1888-1965)

S'io credesse che mia riposta fosse
A persona che mai tornasse al mondo,
Questa fiamma staria senza piu scosse.
Ma perciocche giammai di questo fondo
Non torno vivo alcun, s'i'odo il vero,
Senza tema d'infamia ti rispondo.[1]

Let us go then, you and I,
When the evening is spread out against the sky
Like a patient etherized upon a table:
Let us go, through certain half-deserted streets,
The muttering retreats
Of restless nights in one-night cheap hotels
And sawdust restaurants with oyster-shells :

Streets that follow like a tedious argument
Of insidious intent
To lead you to an overwhelming question...
Oh, do not ask, 'What is it?'
Let us go and make our visit.

In the room the women come and go
Talking of Michelangelo.

The yellow fog that rubs its back upon the window-panes,
The yellow smoke that rubs its muzzle on the window-panes

Licked its tongue into the corners of the evening,
Lingered upon the pools that stand in drains,
Let fall upon its back the soot that falls from chimneys,
Slipped by the terrace, made a sudden leap,
And seeing that it was a soft October night,
Curled once about the house, and fell asleep.

And indeed there will be time
For the yellow smoke that slides along the street
Rubbing its back upon the window-panes;
There will be time, there will be time
To prepare a face to meet the faces that you meet;
There will be time to murder and create,
And time for all the works and days of hands
That life and drop a question on your plate;
Time for you and time for me,
And time yet for a hundred indecisions,

And for hundred visions and revisions,
Before the taking of a toast and tea

In the room the women come and go
Talking of Michelangelo.

And indeed there will be time
To wonder, 'Do I dare?' and, 'Do I dare?'
Time to turn back and descend the stair,
With a bald spot in the middle of my hair —
[They will say : "How his hair is growing thin!]
My morning coat, my collar mounting firmly to the chin,
My necktie rich and modest, but asserted by a simple pin —
[They will say : "But how his arms and legs are thin"]

Do I dare
Disturb the universe?
In a minute there is time
For decisions and revisions which a minute will reverse.

For I have known them already, known them all —
Have known the evenings, mornings, afternoons,

I have measured out my life with coffee spoons;
I know the voices dying with a dying fall
Beneath the music from a farther room.

So how should I presume?

And I have known the eyes already, known them all —
The eyes that fix you in a formulated phrase,
And when I am formulated, sprawling on a pin,

When I am pinned and wriggling on the wall,
Then how should I begin
To spit out all the butt-ends of my days and ways?

And how should I presume?

And I have known the arms already, known them all —
Arms that are braceleted and white and bare
[But in the lamplight, downed with light brown hair!]
Is it perfume from a dress
That makes me so digress?
Arms that lie along a table, or wrap about a shawl.
And should I then presume?
And how should I begin?

... ...

Shall I say, I have gone at dusk through narrow streets
And watched the smoke that rises from the pipes
Of lonely men in shirt-sleeves, leaning out of windows?...
I should have been a pair of ragged claws
Scuttling across the floors of silent seas.

... ...

And the afternoon, the evening, sleeps so peacefully!
Smoothed by long fingers,
Asleep...tired...or it malingers,
Stretched on the floor, here beside you and me.
Should I, after tea and cakes and ices,
Have the strength to force the moment to its crisis?
But though I have wept and fasted, wept and prayed,

Though I have seen my head [grown slightly bald]
brought in upon a platter,
I am no prophet — and here's no great matter;
I have seen the moment of my greatness flicker,
And I have seen the eternal Footman hold my coat, and
snicker,
And in short, I was afraid.

And would it have been worth it, after all,
After the cups, the marmalade, the tea,
Among the porcelain, among some talk of you and me,
Would it have been worth while,
To have bitten off the matter with a smile,
To have squeezed the universe into a ball
To roll it toward some overwhelming question,
To say : 'I am Lazarus, come from the dead,
Come back to tell you all, I shall tell you all' —
If one, settling a pillow by her head,
Should say : 'That is not what I meant at all.
That is not it, at all.'

And would it have been worth it, after all,
Would it have been worth while
After the sunsets and the dooryards and the sprinkled
streets,
After the novels, after the teacups, after the skirts that
Trail along the floor —
And this, and so much more? —
It is impossible to say just what I mean!

But as if a magic lantern threw the nerves in patterns on
a screen :
Would it have been worth while
If one, settling a pillow or throwing off a shawl,
And turning toward the window, should say :
'That is not it at all,
That is not what I meant, at all.'

... ...

No! I am not Prince Hamlet, nor was meant to be;
Am an attendant lord, one that will do
To swell a progress, start a scene or two,
Advise the prince; no doubt, an easy tool,
Deferential, glad to be of use
Politic, cautious, and meticulous;
Full of high sentence, but a bit obtuse;
At times, indeed, almost ridiculous —
Almost, at times, the Fool.

I grow old ... I grow old ...
I shall wear the bottoms of my trousers rolled.

Shall I part my hair behind? Do I dare to eat a peach?
I shall wear white flannel trousers, and walk upon the
beach,
I have heard the mermaids singing, each to each.

I do not think that they will sing to me.

I have seen them riding seaward on the waves
Combing the white hair of the waves blown back

When the wind blows the water white and black.
We have lingered in the chambers of the sea
By sea-girls wreathed with seaweed red and brown
Till human voices wake us, and we drown.

Critical Appreciation

Generally, in his poems, T.S. Eliot dramatizes certain human situations. 'The Love Song of J. Alfred Prufrock' is a dramatization of the tragic predicament of a man who is disillusioned with himself and his society and is unable to find an alternative which can provide him with a meaning in life. His disillusionment leads Prufrock neither to acceptance of the given reality nor to damnation, but to fantasy and daydreaming. Acceptance of the given reality can make life meaningful. Damnation can potentially be the beginning of a new life. Otherwise it has its own meaning, however painful the meaning may be. Fantasy and daydreaming, on the other hand, will only serve ultimately to reinforce the sense of emptiness within. The impossibility of even being damned nullifies the chance for a disillusioned man to turn over a new leaf. As Eliot himself said in his essay on Baudelaire, "damnation itself is an immediate form of Salvation — of Salvation from the ennui of modern life, because it, at least, gives some significance to living." For Eliot the malady that afflicted many of his fellow men was "the inability to be either damned or saved" (D.E.S. Maxwell). Prufrock is a representative of such men.

The epigraph implies that Prufrock lives in a different world, the world of his own hell, a place from which there is no escape. Extracted from Dante's *Inferno,* the epigraph refers to the torture of Guide da Montefeltro in the eighth circle of Hell. His crime is fraud through evil counsel. Prufrock is guilty of a similar crime not because he has perpetrated fraud on others, but because he has deceived himself by perverting his reason as a result of which he lives in his own world of fantasy. In his personal world the only reality is his self. Everything else is seen as an extension of his self. This is the disease of solipsism. Existing in the universe of his own self, "Prufrock can believe in nothing. And believing in nothing, radical skepticism, leads inevitably to solipsism" (J.S. Brooker).

The poem opens with an invitation to a "You" to join the speaker for a walk. The poem being an interior monologue whose function is to reveal the inner movement of consciousness in the mind of a character who lives in his own private world, we may assume that both "You" and "I" stand for Prufrock himself, the two divided selves of Prufrock. The 'I' is the 'willing self', the self that being aware of its tragic situation must take decisions and the 'you' is the complementary part of that self, the 'acting self' which must act according to the decisions taken by the other self. The later half of Prufrock's self is helpless because the former half is impotent to take decisions, to make commitments.

The image in the opening lines makes Prufrock's pathetic situation picturesquely clear. The image is a metaphysical conceit (see Introduction to Metaphysical Poetry, chapter 1) which yokes together the evening and a patient on the one hand, and the sky and the patient's table on the other. The evening is anaesthetized and is lying like a helpless patient on the sprawling sky. This image is extended later on (lines 75-78) when the evening, *i.e.*, Time in which only the consciousness can act, "sleeps so peacefully!" "There is a kinship between Prufrock and the evening," explains Maxwell. Both are apparently peaceful; but it is artificial peace, and there is "an undertone of unhealthiness and unease" in the lines. Maxwell quotes the following lines from Eliot's poem, 'East Cocker,' to illustrate the symbolic connection between ether and the sick mind.

> And you see behind every face the mental emptiness
> deepen
> Leaving only the growing terror of nothing to think about;
> Or when, under ether, the mind is conscious but conscious
> of nothing —

To be "conscious of nothing," to have "nothing to think about" is a symptom of the sick mind. That is Prufrock's horrifying situation. The situation is presented through a series of sordid images : "half-deserted streets," "restless nights in one-night cheap hotels,"[2] "sawdust restaurants with oyster-shells,"[3] and winding streets. Although Prufrock invited his other self to a stroll, he is actually situated in his own room and is fantasizing these images. In other words, these images arise out of his consciousness. They reveal the state of his consciousness not only by their sordidness but also by their lack of stability.

Even if we take them as actual places once frequented by Prufrock, they still reveal his mental condition. Eliot's doctoral thesis was on F.H. Bradley, and idealist philosopher. According to Bradley, one's external sensations are as private to oneself as are his thoughts or his feellings. Every external object has a unique effect on the observer; they become part of the observer's consciousness in a unique way. The sordid, unstable places mentioned are as much part of Prufrock's consciousness as his own identity is.[4] The horror or Prufrock's situation is heightened when we look at these images with reference to the epigraph. Prufrock is in a veritable hell from which there is no escape.

Yet, the places mentioned lead Prufrock to "and overwhelming question." The question is far from articulated;

> Oh, do not ask, 'What is it?'
> Let us go and make our visit.

In the course of the "visit," the journey into his consciousness, the question will become clear. It is not a Hamletean vacillation between 'to be or not to be'; "I am not Prince Hamlet," acknowledges Prufrock (line 111). The question is : 'Do I dare?'

> Do I dare
> Disturb the universe?

This overwhelming question is one of commitment. Can Prufrock rise above his insubstantial fantasies and daydreams, and face squarely the reality in front, however drab and superficial it may be? The reality, Prufrock's social environment, is "inane and stifling and self-satisfied" (Elizabeth Drew). It is represented by the "women (who) come and go/Talking of Michelangelo," by the "some talk of you and me" which is carried out "Among the cups, the marmalade, the tea," by the sunsets, the dooryards, the sprinkled streets, the novels, the skirts, "and so much more." It is a world which gradually withered Prufrock's original nature of intense passion and romantic idealism into defeatism and escapism.

The poem consists of a series of images, some presenting the social environment of which Prufrock is a part, and others revealing his degenerated character. There are some images which serve both the functions. The scenes described, as noted earlier, are both external to and part of Prufrock's consciousness. The fog described in the second section is also part of the psychological landscape of Prufrock. The feline fog goes stealing about closed windows and savours the twilight pleasures of the streets. It

> Licked its tongue into the corners of the evening,
> Lingered upon the pools that stand in drains.

Finally, the gentleness of the October night lulls it to a lazy sleep. In spite of the sexual and sleazy and lassitudinal overtones, this eight-line stanza has a gentle tone and slow rhythm which is in sharp contrast with the harsh tone and faster rhythm of the next twelve lines.

The contrast is not only in tone and rhythm, but in theme too. While the previous stanza is about the death-in-life sterility of the existence without a commitment in an Eliotean waste land, this one is about the pain of the consciousness trying to face the given reality. However, the consciousness is in stupor. Infirm of will, it postpones decision. The phrase, "there will be time" is repeated many times. But the time for the ultimate commitment to life will never come because Prufrock is thinking of accommodating himself to the given social environment. Instead of discovering the deeper recesses of his self and learning to be himself, he will wear masks that suit different occasions : "a face to meet the faces that you meet." And the action will be limited to murder and creation of masks, "a hundred indecisions," "visions and revisions," which will all end with "a toast and tea." All such actions are of no more value than the superficial conversation of women about Michelangelo.

Unable to raise his consciousness above the banality of his social environment, Prufrock postpones the asking of the overwhelming question;

there will be time
To wonder, 'Do I dare?' and, 'Do I dare?'

In his brilliant study on the relationship between Time and Consciousness in Eliot's poems, J.K. Sharma argues that 'The Love song of J. Alfred Prufrock' presents "a duel between time and Consciousness that will not end till its culmination in that triumph of Consciousness over Time which would cost not less than everything." Time is both a creator and a destroyer. It "crushes man's being at every turn but simultaneously confers upon man a means of self-fulfilment." In the case of Prufrock, Time is going to be a destroyer, because instead of making a commitment and thus opening the avenues to self-fulfilment he will "turn back and descend the stair." He becomes self-conscious of his appearance; his baldness and his lean frame. He regards himself as fairly well-dressed. His fear is about the two physical features mentioned. The timidity and self-consciousness prevent him from making a commitment. He would rather leave the "universe" (his environment) and its laws to themselves and take shelter in opportunistic decisions.

Having tried to face the reality and failed, Prufrock once again reverts to defeatism. His excuse is that having "known them all already" there is no reason for him to hope for a better, a meaningful existence. His experience has been such that he has no reason to look forward with hope to a life of any significance. He lived a tediously monotonous life "measuring out his life with coffee spoons." The voices, the eyes and the arms are all familiar to him, and he knows that they will not be of any help in raising him out of his self-pity and "soul-dampness" (Maxwell's phrase). The voices will die "with a dying fall/Beneath the music from a farther room." The eyes will fix him in a formula. Thus he will be given his place in the conventional order. He will be classified like an insect that is pinned on the wall. This prejudiced classification will prevent him from making any new commitment in life which demands a break with the past. As he thinks of the arms he is distracted for a while, by erotic thoughts. He wonders whether it is the "perfume from a dress" that makes him digress. As George Williamson asks, "is it a digression?" The whole part speaking about arms has a sexual undertone.

All the three images mentioned in this part of the poem serve a specific function each. The dying voices indicate the futility of an attempt to make a meaningful communication; the eyes that fix one in a preconceived formula imply that one cannot easily escape one's past; and the arms show the shallowness of sexual relationships. Bereft of meaning and depth, the experiences cannot lead Prufrock to a commitment, to turning over a new leaf. Hence the query : "how should I begin?"

Prufrock indicates that his experiences are not unique. He has seen enough of other men like him while he went walking through narrow streets at dusk. If loneliness, frustration and meaninglessness are what life can offer, it would be better to be "a pair of ragged claws" in the sea. That is, he would rather be a creature without the painful consciousness. Or, in the words of Elizabeth Drew, "his secret wish is only to regress to a safe haven where his inner universe is no longer disturbed by any tormenting human problems." This desire is born of Prufrock's abject self-pity and self-disgust which render him incapable of making a commitment.

The man incapable of making a commitment is the patient who sleeps under the effect of ether at the beginning of the poem. As has already been stated, the external objects are seen by Prufrock as extensions of his own self. The evening, which is also an extension of Prufrock's self, is mentioned again now after Prufrock expresses his helpless desire to escape from his consciousness. The weariness of the evening is Prufrock's own weariness. He lacks "the strength to force the moment to its crisis." This is capitulation of the self.

Prufrock thinks of certain great persons who found meaning in life through a total self-surrender. The line, "I have wept and fasted, wept and prayed," refers to Jesus' mental agony before submitting himself to the will of God. Prufrock compares himself to John the Baptist whose head was "brought in upon a platter." John the Baptist was beheaded because he was committed unconditionally to a cause, to certain principles. Commitment to a cause demands surrender of the self to the natural flow of reality of which the self is a part. Such commitment may lead one to a tragic end as in the case of Jesus and John the Baptist. Prufrock foresees such a possible end to himself if he makes the commitment :

> And I have seen the eternal Footman[5] hold my coat,
> and snicker.

Admitting his fear of this possible end, Prufrock refuses to commit himself to life.

Prufrock would have been as great as the prophet or Jesus if only he could face the moment of crisis and surpass it. But "he denies his self the freedom to choose to become a being other than what he has already been" (J.K. Sharma). Hence he sees "the moment of his greatness flicker."

Having chosen defeat, or, being unable to face reality, Prufrock begins to rationalize his failure. The question, "Would it have been worth-while?" is repeated many times. Prufrock wonders weather a belated act of commitment would have changed his life at all. His fear is that of being misunderstood. Making a commitment is equal to raising his self out of its burial in his own consciousness. The universe that Prufrock would have squeezed into a ball is the world of his own self. Suppose he mustered up enough courage to let his self encounter an overwhelming question, encounter reality. He would then receive a new life as Lazarus did when he was resurrected by Jesus. Lazarus did not speak anything about his life in the other world. But if Prufrock were to speak of his previous life, would he not be misunderstood? In short, he rationalizes his lack of courage and takes shelter in flimsy excuses.

Apart from mere rationalization, there is also a genuine problem that Prufrock faces : the problem of communication. "It is impossible to say just what I mean!" he admits. Can any person reveal himself fully to another? If that is an impossibility, how can one expect to be accepted as he is? This is a genuine problem to the idealist in Prufrock. He is aware that he can only reveal himself partially much as he may wish to go beyond the "patterns on a screen" and reveal his real self. Such partial revelation is destined to lead to misunderstandings. Hence the whole effort may not be "worth it after all."

The problem of communication is a theme common to much of Eliot's poetry. Since communication between one person and another is difficult, individuals are often destined to live in isolation. Prufrock is unable to communicate clearly. He offers us glimpses into his personal universe. The poem is like a series of slides, as Unger says. "Each slide is an isolated, fragmentary images, producing its own effect, including suggestions of some larger actions or situation of which it is but an arrested moment." Unger argues that each part of the poem is both fragmentary and whole, and that Prufrock's own nature is not different. He does not ever reveal his entire self.

Prufrock is unable to reveal his entire self because the self has been disintegrated gradually. It is the disintegration, coupled witn Prufrock's lack of will to come to terms with his situation that leads him to "a hundred visions and revisions." However, he acknowledges that he is not Hamlet. Because he cannot rise to tragic heights. He regards himself as more comparable to Polonius, an attendant who plays many roles that suit different occasions.

Prufrock becomes self-conscious once again. He is concerned about his growing old. He leaves aside thoughts of any significance and dallies with such questions as : "Shall I part my hair behind? Do I dare to eat a peach?"

Unable to encounter the critical moment, Prufrock first sinks to banal considerations and then to delusion. He thinks of mermaids singing to each other and dismisses the possibility of their singing to him. His earlier attempts at establishing relationships with women have not been successful. The women "talking of Michelangelo" did not appeal to him. The women in his past experiences have not been very promising as far as establishment of meaningful relationships is concerned. His entire past has been a failure. But if he speaks frankly about it now, he may only be misunderstood and that is a forbidding prospect. He would rather delude himself by fantasizing about the mermaids.

Prufrock is a person who has lived his life with a counterfeit personality. He refused to be himself. He failed to see himself as an organic part of the infinite reality that life and the nature constitute. Instead he viewed himself as some kind of absolute entity to which everything is subservient. The natural consequence of such an approach to the reality external to the self is eventual breakdown of the self on the realization of its hollowness. In the words of J.K. Sharma, "Prufrock's life signifies, if anything it signifies at all, the inauthenticity of existence, or 'timidity' to face the critical situation."

Nevertheless, Prufrock is a man who has a desire somewhere deep within himself to emerge out of his self and establish relationship with the external reality. That is why he calls his song a "Love Song." But this desire is impotent because Prufrock is incapable of action. He will be able to act only when he becomes an authentic person, when he frees himself from delusions and accepts himself and the external reality as they are.

1. Literal translation of the epigraph : If I thought that my answer were to one who ever could return to the world; this flame should quake no more : but since none ever did return from this depth, if what I hear be true, without fear of infamy I answer thee.
2. This image suggests loveless unsatisfying sexual relationships.
3. Cheap restaurants having shell ashtrays.
4. "A person's identity is defined by his world, and to escape one is as difficult as to escape the other," says Leonard Unger referring to the Bradleyan philosophy.
5. In the Hindu mythology, Yama, god of death, has four footmen who are sent to carry the spirit of the man who dies.

20

The Whitsun Weddings

PHILIP LARKIN

That whitsun, I was late getting away:
    Not till about
One — twenty on the sunlit Saturday
Did my three-quarters-empty train pull out,
Al windows down, all cushions hot, all sense
Of being in a hurry gone. We ran
Behind the backs of houses, crossed a street.
Of blinding windscreens, smelt the fish-dock; thence
The river's level drifting breadth began,
Where sky and Lincolnshire and water meet.

All afternoon, through the tall heat that slept
    For miles inland,
A slow and stopping curve southwards we kept.
Wide farms went by, short-shadowed cattle, and
Canals with floatings of industrial froth;
A hothouse flashed uniquely: hedges dipped
And rose : and now and then a smell of grass
Displaced the reek of buttoned carriage-cloth
Until the next town, new and nondescript,
Approached with acres of dismantled cars.

At first, I didn't notice what a noise
    The weddings made
Each station that we stopped at : sun destroys
The interest of what's happening in the shade,

And down the long cool platforms whoops and skirls
I took for porters larking with the mails,
And went on reading. Once we started, though,
We passed them, grinning and pomaded, girls
In parodies of fashion, heels and veils,
All posed irresolutely, watching us go,

As if out on the end of an event
    Waving goodbye
To something that survived it. Struck, I leant
More promptly out next time, more curiously,
And saw it all again in different terms:
The fathers with broad belts under their suits
And seamy foreheads; mothers loud and fat;
An uncle shouting smut; and then the perms,
The nylon gloves and jewellery-substitutes,
The lemons, mauves, and olive-ochres that

Marked off the girls un-really from the rest.
    Yes, from cafes
And banquet-halls up yards, and bunting-dressed
Coach-party annexes, the wedding-days
Were coming to an end. All down the line
Fresh couples climbed aboard : the rest stood round;
The last confetti and advice were thrown,
And, as we moved, each face seemed to define
Just what it saw departing: children frowned
At something dull; fathers had never known

Success so huge and wholly farcical;
    The women shared
The secret like a happy funeral;
While girls, gripping their handbags tighter, stared
At a religious wounding. Free at last,
And loaded with the sum of all they saw,
We hurried towards London, shuffling gouts of steam.
Now fields were building-plots, and poplars cast
Long shadows over major roads, and for
Some fifty minutes, that in time would seem,

Just long enough to settle hats and say
I nearly died,
A dozen marriages got under way.
They watched the landscape, sitting side by side
— An Odeon went past, a cooling tower,
And someone running up to bowl — and none
Thought of the others they would ever meet
Or how their lives would all contain this hour.
I thought of London spread out in the sun,
Its postal districts packed like squares of wheat :

There we were aimed. And as we raced across
Bright knots of rail
Past standing Pullmans, walls of blackened moss
Came close, and it was nearly done, this frail
Travelling coincidence; and what it held
Stood ready to be loosed with all the power
That being changed can give. We slowed again,
And as the tightened brakes took hold, there swelled
A sense of falling, like an arrow-shower
Sent out of sight, somewhere becoming rain.

Critical Appreciation

Philip Larkin is one of the Movement poets (see Introduction to Twentieth Century Poetry, p. 99). He believed that "every poem must be its own freshly created universe." If each poem is a universe by itself, it obviously means that it does not rely on any tradition external to it for enhancing its meaning or value. Larkin was, for this reason, opposed even to making allusions to other poems or poets in his own poems. He also strove against obscurities and irrationalities in poems. His attempt is to see things as they are. Hence, the symbolic mode is also unacceptable to him. He emphasizes the superiority of content over technique. The result is that his poems are realistic pictures of ordinary life.

Clarity and elegance are two virtues conspicuous in Larkin's poems. He observes the details with the interest of a novelist. In most of his poems, the poetic person is a careful observer of the behavior of himself and others. This observer is a detached person who is usually moved deeply by what he sees. His response to the observed reality is sensitive in spite of the touches of irony.

The irony may be an offshoot of Larkin's worldview. Larkin sees the world as moving "in accordance with an inexorable and unconscious law whose goal is just the movement."* It is a blind movement, endless cycles of generation and extinction. There is nothing spiritual about it. The terms 'good' and 'evil' have no meaning except in man's mind. The consciousness of good and evil does not make man great, though. On the contrary, Larkin "sees humanity as small, unheroic, selfish, anxious, pathetic and conflicted."

The conflict is between consciousness of the ideal and knowledge of reality, and it is the essence of human nature, according to Larkin. Nature, being a blind force, as noted earlier, recognizes no individual ideals. Society is also "a force analogous to nature in its pervasiveness and power, its ability to 'ruin' and its impassivity and unconcern for the plight of the individual." Individual ideals are no concern of the society either.

It does not mean, however, that the individual with all his ideals is great. Like humanity itself, the individual man too has many a limitation. He shares the limitations of his species. Some of the drawbacks revealed by Larkin's individual characters are selfishness, passivity, short-sightedness, ruthlessness, defensiveness and envy. But these vices lose their sting when Larkin tells us that the individual is also the victim of a cruel joke enacted by the invulnerable nature, which is itself controlled by a mightier and incomprehensible force, *viz.*, fate. Hence, Larkin views man with sympathy.

Larkin's view of man and his world endows him with a pragmatic and ironic outlook on the events of daily life. We can see such an outlook coupled with sympathy in 'The Whitsun Weddings,' the title poem of his 1964 collection. The poem is about the newly married couples whom the poet or the narrator sees as he travels by train from Hull to London on a Saturday, and the impact made on him by the sight.

The first two stanzas describe the panorama of the British urban and rural scenes as a train moves through them with varying speeds. The scenes are like snapshots taken at random. They reveal to us, wide farms with cattle grazing on them, "canals with floatings of industrial froth," a hothouse, hedges, dumping ground of dismantled cars, and so on. The narrator is also conscious of certain smells such as that from a fish-dock or of grass. The scenes and smells, casually sensed rather than carefully observed, signify the very nature of life itself: a random mixture of the good and the bad. The negative side of industrialization is also hinted at. Larkin was conscious of the emptiness of the mechanical age.

From stanza 3, onwards the poem presents with exact detail, a human drama enacted on the train and the platforms of the railway stations. We may say that there are three stages in the drama. These stages are with respect to the narrator of the poem. The first is that of sensory perception (stanza 3), followed by curious interest (stanzas 4-6), and ending in active cognition or participation in the drama (stanzas 7-8). Like most of Larkin's poems, this one is also cumulative in effect. Starting with a casual presentation of natural scenes, 'The Whitsun Weddings' moves through a distanced observation to some kind of a participation in the human activity presented.

In stanza 3, the narrator is a detached observer. Significantly, the activity at this stage has not yet become part of the train journey but takes place on the station platforms. The narrator does not initially notice the "noise" made by the weddings. The afternoon sun is too hot to induce interest in anything in particular. So the narrator goes on reading until the train starts from a certain station when he begins to notice the people on the platforms. They look as if they were

> out on the end of an event.
> Waving goodbye.
> To something that survived it.

For the first time there is a touch of direct metaphor in the poem. The narrator is passing from the stage of sensory perception to that of curious interest. He begins to perceive more than what the senses reveal. Upto this point of time, the narrator has been an outsider, "not in sympathy with the world exterior to himself, regarding that world as a parade of surfaces, flat, de-spirited objective phenomena." At this point, he is beginning to participate in the symbolic meaning of the wedding ceremony. The ceremony itself is over. But a new life is beginning for the couples.

Larkin's expression, "...waving goodbye/To something that survived it," has a touch of irony. In the context of the poem what survives the "event" of the wedding ceremony is the married life, and the people on the platform are waving goodbye to the new couples who are on their honeymoon trip. In other words, now they are left to themselves. It is upto them to make of their lives what they will, though they will not be free from the inexorable powers of fate. Whether the married life will be happy and fruitful is unknown, although it has started on a jubilant note. This irony will reach its climax with greater depth of meaning in the concluding stanza.

At the moment the narrator is still and observer, though not a disinterested one as earlier. He distinguishes individual faces in the crowd : fathers, mothers, and uncle. He also notices the girls' nylon gloves and jewellery substitutes as well as the distinct colours of their dresses. He visualizes wedding halls and cafes. Even the facial expressions of the people attract his attention. He sees children frowning, fathers roaring with laughter, mothers sharing both joy and sorrow (sorrow, because their daughters are leaving them), and young girls being hopeful about their own marriages. This close observation is the result of the increasing active interest taken by the narrator in the event that is unfolding before him.

In the second half of the sixth stanza the train draws closer to London. The vast fields give way to buildings and wide roads become visible. The narrator's attention focuses on the newly married couples. They "sitting side by side" watch the landscape outside. A new life is beginning for each of them. None of the couples think of the others. They have all been brought together by accident, by "this frail/Travelling coincidence."

The narrator tries to interpret his experience in the last stanza. He was a detached observer in the beginning. The "three-quarters-empty train" is a metaphor for the narrator's own initial psychological condition. As the train moves through time and space, the narrator's weary emptiness gets filled. The heat of the sun and the sordidness of the sights outside are insignificant now. Just as "this hour" of the train journey will be a memorable one for the couples, the experience will be memorable to the poet too. He has been filled with "the power/That being changed can give."

The power is a boon of his intense experience. The train journey has somehow been a metaphor for life itself. It united such antitheses as "continuation and change, the unique and the generic, the self and others. The twentieth century with its trains, perms, and industrial froth links with past generations of marriages that have taken place traditionally on that day."

In other words, the one hour of the rain journey has provided the poet with a peculiar experience, that of life itself.

However, Larkin is not an idealist. His most regular stance is that of "a simple ordinary man in an unromantic world." He is a realist. Reality is what we see around us, while ideals are what we imagine and desire. The conflict between reality and ideal is unavoidable. While construction of the ideal is normal, belief in it, is a lie. This leads to the irony in Larkin's poems. It is this irony that we detect in the last stanza of 'The Whitsun Weddings.' In the words of Michael Kirkham :

> Life becomes, in a half-facetiously reclaimed metaphor, a voyage, but one without significant coherence : the sights of Odeon, cooling tower and cricket match go by in random sequence; their destination is something as blankly impersonal as a map of London's postal districts. Comparing the districts to 'squares of wheat,' a harvest neatly packaged, the poet, out of charity, conjures the ghost of a possible fulfilment, but withholds the reality in a concluding stanza all along delicately poised between hope and failure.

The climax of the irony is in the imagery of the "arrow-shower" in the concluding lines of the poem. The married life that is just beginning for the couples may bear fruit somewhere some time. It will be decided by destiny which has the potential to shatter human ideals and desires. But there is room for hope yet.

Larkin's talent for orderly arrangement and formal perfection are reflected in the poem. The structure of the poem is firm. The stanzas have a polished rhyme scheme : ababcdecde. The diction is polished too, though prosaic.

---

* All the unacknowledged quotations which are not from the poem itself are from Lolette Kuby, *An Uncommon Poet for the Common Man : A Study of Philip Larkin's Poetry*.

21

Hawk Roosting

TED HUGHES (1932-1998)

I sit in the top of the wood, my eyes closed.
Inaction, no falsifying dream
Between my hooked head and hooked feet:
Or in sleep rehearse perfect kills and eat.

The convenience of the high trees!
The air's buoyancy and the sun's ray
Are of advantage to me;
And the earth's face upward for my inspection.

My feet are locked upon the rough bark.
It took the whole of Creation
To produce my foot, my each feather :
Now I hold Creation in my foot

Or fly up, and revolve it all slowly —
I kill, where I please, because it is all mine.
There is no sophistry in my body :
My manners are tearing off heads —

The allotment of death.
For the one path of my flight is direct
Through the bones of the living.
No arguments assert my right;

The sun is behind me.
Nothing has changed since I began.
My eye has permitted no change.
I am going to keep things like this.

Critical Appreciation

'Hawk Roosting' is one of the animal poems in Hughes's second collection of poems, *Lupercal*, published in 1960. Most of the animal poems in Hughes's first two collections celebrate the primitive vitality in Nature; the animals rely solely on their pristine instincts and revel in them.

The hawk in 'Hawk Roosting' is an embodiment of the life of pristine instinct. It sits "in the top of the wood" like the lord of the earth and tells us about its life of instinct, life 'uncorrupted' by "falsifying dreams" which are nurtured by reason and civilization. Its eyes are closed to the faculties of the mind, which corrupt elemental life. It is our body, not the mind that is alive to instinct. The hawk acts purely by instinct. The activity is predatory and the hawk's entire body, from head to foot (both of which are qualified as "hooked," emphasizing the predatory nature), is adapted to that activity. Even its dreams are about preying. The bird makes no bones about its nature. Refusing absolutely to indulge in sophistry, it states bluntly :

> My manners are tearing off heads —
> The allotment of death.
> For the one path of my flight is direct
> Through the bones of the living.

Its right to kill, does not require the moral support sustained by logical arguments. That right is in its blood. The bird has been living according to its nature ever since it was born. As far as it is concerned, its life will always go on the same way.

The hawk in the poem is not merely a preying bird that gives free play to its instinct; it is positively blood-thirsty. It gloats over its ability to "hold Creation in its foot" and to cut "Through the bones of the living." Furthermore, it is a narcissist. Alan Bold calls it "a complete solipsist" (*Thom Gunn and Ted Hughes*). It views itself as God's supreme creation; its world is the world it sees; it believes that everything exists for its sake; and it is equal to God in its role as arbiter of death. Its narcissism or solipsism is part of its god-likeness.

Thus, the hawk combines in it three things: life of instinct, brutality and god-likeness. All these three things are aspects of

Nature's vitality itself. That Hughes saw all these in the hawk, is obvious from his own view of the poem expressed in an interview :

> What I had in mind was that in this hawk Nature is thinking. Simply Nature. It's not so simple may be because Nature is no longer simple. I intended some Creator like the Jehovah of Job but more feminine. When Christianity kicked the devil out of Job what they actually kicked out was Nature... and nature became the devil. He doesn't sound like Isis, mother of the gods, which he is. He sounds like Hitler's familiar spirit.

'Hawk Roosting,' like most poems of Hughes, celebrates the vital energy of Nature to the extent of being anti-human. Hughes is opposed to man's total neglect of his animal appetites, his primal energy. This neglect has created a vacuum in man. The evolution of man has been one-sided: intellectual. This sapped the enormous vital energy of the creature called man who is in fact both rational and passionate, both mind and body. The neglect of the body, caused mostly by man's fear of its brutal energy, is what makes nature "no longer simple." It is not Nature that has become complex, but man who created a split within him between mind and body, between reason and instinct. Man has been suppressing his instincts. Drawing on Freudian Psychology, Hughes argues in his essay "Myth and Education" (1970) that the suppression leads to disease. Modern man is suffering from a self-inflicted disease, a disease inflicted by his excessive cerebration.

The ancient wise men created rituals and dogma which contained the violent energy that man inherited from Nature. In an interview to *London Magazine* (Jan 1971), Hughes says that modern man has lost faith in the old rituals and dogma, but has not found any alternative which can contain the violent energy. Hence he suppresses this energy into the deep recesses of the unconscious by different means such as rationalization and philosophisation. The more suppressed an evil, the more devilish it becomes. Thus while animals revel in their pristine energy instinctively, man suppresses it and makes a devil of it.

In an interview to *Guardian* (1965), Hughes said, "My poems are not about violence but vitality." He meant the vitality of elemental life. Man's increasing alienation from that vitality is a major concern of Hughes. In the same interview, Hughes described the animals in his poems as "living the redeemed life of joy." It is that joy that man is deprived of. This joy can only come as a result of man's genuine contact with his instincts. In practical terms it means perfect adaptation to the needs of life and total absorption of being in action (Terry Gifford and Neil Roberts, *Ted Hughes : A Critical Study*). The hawk in 'Hawk Roosting' is in possession of such joy. Nevertheless, we cannot ignore the obvious brutality of the hawk. As implied earlier, this brutality too is part of Nature. Is Hughes then asking us to let our hair down and revel in our animal instincts like Mr. Hyde so that we too shall live "the redeemed life of joy?"

Thomas West's answer to this question is : "In a way, one could say that all of Ted Hughes's poetry is a variation on the Dr Jekyll and My Hyde theme, with this twist : Hyde, the body and repulsive toad, is the real possessor of knowledge, and Jekyll, the enlightened or sophisticated mind, is the guilt-ridden, accused party" (*Ted Hughes*). In other words, Mr. Hyde is justified in-so-far as he is in touch with his instincts, and Dr. Jekyll is guilty in-so-far as he is out of touch with them. The problem, then, is the body-mind or instinct-intellect split in the modern man. The remedy, suggests Hughes (in his essay, 'Myth and Education,' 1970), is to welcome "the devil of the suppressed life" back into consciousness. "The best way to welcome him and to release him...is within the framework of a fantasy."

That is exactly what Hughes is doing in 'Hawk Roosting'. The blood-thirsty, violently energetic hawk is indeed "the devil of the suppressed life" of the poet, of the civilized man, that is brought back into consciousness and released within the framework of the poem. Thus the poem has a cathartic value. It brings the reader face to face with a being that is forbiddingly instinctual, and lets him encounter the suppressed part of his own self.

In form, the poem is an interior monologue. The diction with its harsh sounds suits the theme of violent energy. The rhythm as well as the poetic images are both attracting and repelling at once just as the primal energy of the hawk is both attractive and repulsive. The note of ominousness in the last lines is particularly striking.

Thomas West points out that one of the major natural influences on the young Hughes was a steep cliff, Scout Rock, in Calder Valley where the poet grew up as a boy. It was believed that the cliff had an evil eye so that it evoked irresistible suicidal thoughts in the beholder. The dangerous cliff seemed to lure the beholder like a vicious but enchanting siren. It was at once attractive and repulsive. One could counter the suicidal thought by viewing the cliff as a challenge as an adventurous mountaineer would do. Commenting on this West says that "the alternatives when faced with an...obstacle of a natural form are extinction or conquest." The hawk, like the Scout Rock, like Nature itself, is both luring and ominous. Hughes has succeeded in capturing the entire vital spirit of nature in the poem.

Bibliography

Anderson, Warren D. 1988. *Matthew Arnold and the Classical Tradition*. University of Michigan, Michigan.

Bennett, Joan. 1988. *Five Metaphysical Poets*. Radha Publishing House, Calcutta.

Bloom, Harold. 1970. *Yeats*. Oxford University Press, London.

Bold, Alan. 1976. *Thom Gunn and Ted Hughes*. Oliver and Boyd, Edinburgh.

Bowra, Maurice. 1961. *The Romantic Imagination*. Oxford University Press, Oxford.

Brooke, Stoppard A. 1985. *Tennyson : His Art and Relation to Modern Life*. Aparna Publications, Delhi.

Bush, Douglas. 1965. *English Poetry : the Main Currents from Chaucer to the Present*. Methuen, London.

Butt, J. 1979 (1990). *Age of Johnson 1740-1789* (ed. Carnall, Geoffrey). Oxford University Press, Oxford.

Crowell, Norton B. 1963. *The Triple Soul : Browning's Theory of Knowledge*. University of New Mexico, New Mexico.

Dickstein, Morris. 1971. *Keats and His Poetry* : A Study in Development. University of Chicago Press, Chicago.

Dixon, Peter (ed.). 1972. *Alexander Pope*. Ohio University Press, Ohio.

Dowden, Edward. 1969. *Life of Percy Bysshe Shelley*. Routledge and Kegan Paul, London.

Drew, Elizabeth. 1993. *T.S. Eliot : The Design of His Poetry*. Doaba House, New Delhi.

Durrant, Geoffrey. 1969. *William Wordsworth*. Cambridge University Press.

Dyson, A.E. (ed.). 1990. *Three Contemporary Poets : Thom Gunn, Ted Hughes and R.S. Thomas : a casebook*. Macmillan, Houndmills.

Dyson, A.E. & Lovelock, Julian. 1976. *Masterful Images : English Poetry from Metaphysicals to Romantics*. Macmillan, London.

Flowers, Betty S. 1976. *Browning and the Modern Tradition*. Macmillan, London.

Gifford, Terry & Robert, Neil. 1981. *Ted Hughes : A Critical Study*. Faber and Faber, London.

Gridley, Roy E. 1972. *Browning*. Routledge and Kegan Paul, London.

Hartman, Geoffrey H. 1980. *Hopkins : A Collection of Critical Essays*. Prentice-Hall of India, New Delhi.

Hough, Graham. 1967. *The Romantic Poets*. Hutchinson, London.

Jack, Ian. 1973. *Browning's Major Poetry*. Clarendon Press, Oxford.

——. 1967. *Keats and the Mirror of Art*. Clarendon Press, Oxford.

Jump, J.D. (ed.). 1965. Introduction to *Matthew Arnold : Prose Selection*. Macmillan, London.

Keats, John. 1965. *Letters of John Keats*. University of London Press, London.

Kuby Lolette. 1974. *Uncommon Poet for the Common Man : A Study of Philip Larkin's Poetry*. Mouton, The Hague.

Leighton, A. 1954 (1976). *Shelley and the Sublime : An Interpretation of the Major Poems*. Cambridge University Press, Cambridge.

Martz, Louis. 1954 (1976). *Poetry of Meditation : A Study in English Literature of the Seventeenth Century*. Yale University Press, New Haven.

Maxwell, D.E.S. 1960. *The Poetry of T.S. Eliot*. Routledge and Kegan Paul, London.

Miller, J. Hillis in Hartman, G.H. (ed.). pp. 89-116.

Miner, Earl. 1974. *Restoration Mode from Milton to Dryden*. Princeton University Press, Princeton.

Pattison, Robert. 1979. *Tennyson and Tradition*. Harvard University Press, Cambridge.

Sharma, Jitendra Kumar. 1985. *Time and T.S. Eliot : His Poetry, Plays and Philosophy*. Sterling, New Delhi.

Unger, Leonard. 1966. *T.S. Eliot : Moments and Patterns*. University of Minneapolis, Minneapolis.

Ward, Aileen. 1966. *John Keats : The Making of a Poet*. Mercury Books, London.

Wasserman, Earl R. 1967. *The Finer Tone : Keats' Major Poems*. John Hopkins Press, Baltimore.

West, Thomas. 1985. *Ted Hughes*. Methuen, London.

Williamson, George. 1967. *A Reader's Guide to T.S. Eliot : A Poem-by-poem analysis*. Thames and Hudson, London.

Wilson, F.A.C. 1968. *W.B. Yeats and Tradition :* Methuen, London.